THE

MEETING

BOOK

PAUL M. ENGLISH

THE
MEETING
BOOK

HOW THE *Best*
COMPANIES
Meet BETTER

WILEY

Published by John Wiley & Sons, Inc., Hoboken, New Jersey.

For general information on our other products and services or for technical support, please contact our Customer Care Department within the United States at (800) 762-2974, outside the United States at (317) 572-3993 or fax (317) 572-4002.

Wiley also publishes its books in a variety of electronic formats. Some content that appears in print may not be available in electronic formats. For more information about Wiley products, visit our web site at www.wiley.com.

Library of Congress Cataloging-in-Publication Data:

ISBN: 9781394391790 (hardback)
ISBN: 9781394391806 (ePub)
ISBN: 9781394391813 (ePDF)

COVER DESIGN: PAUL MCCARTHY
COVER ART: © GETTY IMAGES | PIRANKA
Printed and bound by CPI Group (UK) Ltd, Croydon, CR0 4YY

C9781394391790_020426

To Rachel, Nicole, Michael, Ed, Eileen, Tim, Nancy, Dan, and Barbara, and their families. I love you to the end of the earth.

And to the many teams I've worked with and learned from over my technology and nonprofit careers. I'm a better leader and person due to every one of you.

Contents

Introduction

"**M**eetings are the worst part of my job." "Most of my meetings are bad, a waste of time for everyone in the room." "Meetings are the death of productivity." These are the all-too-common refrains that you hear about company gatherings large and small.

Disdain for meetings is so pervasive that it has spawned a subgenre of office humor and de-motivational posters: Let's have a meeting to discuss the things that must happen but never actually will. The world is run by people able to sit there until the end of all meetings. Are you lonely? Tired of working on your own? Hate making decisions? Hold a meeting. See other people. Show charts. Point with a stick. Feel important. Eat donuts. All on company time.

The evidence that bad meetings are costly and are quietly killing your company is everywhere. Just look at the 93 million professional workers in the United States who consistently report in surveys that they spend 30% of their work time in meetings, and that half of their meetings are "bad." That works out to six hours of bad meetings per week. With the average US salary at $30 per hour, the cost of bad meetings per week is an astounding $16.7 billion. In a year, that's $870 billion, which equals 3% of the US gross domestic product, laid to waste, not just as lost time, but more importantly, as lost opportunity.

When meetings have no clear agenda, when too many people are invited, when people come unprepared, when people are rude and interrupt one another, when there are no action items and no decisions made, when the meeting starts late or runs too long, or when there are simply too many meetings, your company and its culture suffer way more than meets the eye. But it doesn't have to be that way.

In 2012, when my cofounder and I sold our 200-employee startup Kayak for $2 billion and we became a business unit of the world's largest online travel company, everyone wanted to know: How did you do that? How did you achieve $1.5 million in annual revenue per employee? The answer I always give is that we focused on two things: (1) we hired the best people and (2) the way we ran meetings.

This book will teach you how to improve meetings and why the best companies meet better. It's based on what I learned from running about 20,000 meetings over the years. I've seen how cultivating a strong meeting culture helps you get the most out of your people by enriching their experience and effectiveness. Despite the cynicism that surrounds meetings in many companies, great meetings can be super productive and even joyful!

Especially if you commit to holding fewer meetings, smaller ones, and shorter ones. High-impact meetings can be the secret key to building a successful organization.

I became maniacal about meetings early in my career in the software industry. After I sold my first software startup to Intuit in the late 1990s, I joined what was then a 7,000-employee company that had already established a strong meeting culture and was open to allowing me to bring my belief in holding smaller, shorter, fewer, and better meetings to the larger enterprise. I tell the story of that experience and what I learned as a foundational case study in building a strong meeting culture.

I've also had opposite experiences. A more recent software startup that I sold to a giant financial company had me joining the new parent full-time and attending endless strings of meetings that made me lose the will to work. And so I quit, specifically because of all the bad meetings.

My own journey through company meeting cultures is joined by telling stories of other examples of successful companies—including Amazon, Airbnb, Intuit, OpenTable, and LinkedIn—that contribute key learnings that you can and must put into practice in your organization. Whereas Part I of the book tracks the narratives of how a strong meeting culture was a critical success factor for each, Part II extracts the principles, tips, and action steps to make them accessible to any organization.

The reason I draw most of my case stories from high-tech companies is not just because I know this world the best. It's also because tech has been the world's most dynamic and fastest growing industry for decades now. By interviewing the founders and leaders of those companies, I can impart the inside stories in a way that shows the causes and effects of building a strong meeting culture. The companies chosen here are the ones that have come to dominate their markets, and it's the quality of their meetings that makes them efficient, smart, innovative, and successful.

What's more, the meeting itself has been transformed by technology. Sometimes too much. Presentation software is probably the best-known culprit. The phrase "death by PowerPoint" refers to how substituting a series of prepared slides often makes everyone's eyes glaze over and tune out. When the global COVID-19 pandemic hit, meetings shifted to Zoom and other online conferencing tools almost instantaneously. As a result, it became easier than ever to set up and pack more meetings into weekly schedules. It got to the point where millions of workers would dread opening their calendars only to see an endless stretch of meetings.

We've now entered the era of artificial intelligence (AI). The book builds toward the opening of that era and what it means for meetings, how the technology can be deployed to transform both the scheduling of meetings and the analysis of meetings in order to get the most out of the time humans gather together. But the essential endeavor of running a great meeting is at its core a purely human effort.

AI on its own cannot fix a broken meeting culture, and indeed could make it much worse. It's why you must focus on the underlying meeting culture at your company at the human level in order to get ready for the ways that AI can make meetings even more effective. Indeed, when meetings are regularly transcribed and summarized by the large language models (LLMs) of AI, that trove can become your largest and most valuable dataset.

The wisdom in this book applies equally to in-person meetings, online meetings, and hybrid meetings. Companies must find the best mix that works for them. Whatever the setting, holding great meetings is the best way to confront pressing conflicts, present information-rich road maps, set lofty goals, make high-stakes decisions, and get your people energized to help transform your company via growth and innovation. By providing a combination of evocative narratives and a distillation of best meeting practices, my wish is to ensure that you never look at meetings the same way again.

PART I

Stories

CHAPTER 1

How Intuit Became a Master of Meetings

In the beginning, meetings were not considered key to the culture at Intuit Inc. Founded in the 1980s by former Procter & Gamble manager Scott Cook, the startup that would one day become one of world's 100 most valuable companies began with an idea Scott got when his wife, Signe, kept complaining about the time-consuming and disorganized process of paying their bills. Intuit's first development team operated out of Silicon Valley offices featuring the obligatory foosball table and unlimited sodas and snacks to fuel coding binges by young software engineers. Meetings were informal, mostly unplanned. The team was focused on a clear goal and driven by the promise of stock options. For a stretch of six months, the venture ran out of funds, and everyone worked without pay.

When it came to launching Quicken, Intuit's flagship personal finance package, Cook insisted on being highly disciplined, going so far as to hold up a stopwatch while observing customers using the software to print out checks. There were competing programs on the shelf at software shops and electronics stores. But Quicken, as the fastest and simplest, captured 80% of the market as one of the first generation of "killer apps" of the personal computer era. Cook attributed this early success to a relentless focus on the customer. "We're a consumer products company," Cook told *BusinessWeek* in 1991. "The word software isn't used when we define our mission."

Intuit began to create a high-impact meetings culture almost by accident. "We backed into it," Cook says nowadays. As modems first became available, it was possible to pay bills online, leading to countless meetings with financial institutions curious about the benefits of linking Quicken to bank accounts. More meetings were needed to decide what other areas of personal finance to explore. After Intuit's initial public offering on the Nasdaq, scrutiny and pressures within the company intensified. Intuit used its stock to acquire a little-known program called TurboTax that was struggling to find footing in the market. Intuit had to figure out what to do with it.

Meetings defaulted to PowerPoint presentations by top executives that drew blind praise from programmers who rarely spoke up about what was on their minds. Such meetings weren't an honest confrontation of challenges. Instead, Cook came to see these unproductive sessions as bottlenecks preventing progress and growth.

Cook identified a set of "meetings maladies." Boring. One-way. Lack of discussion. Lack of participation. Lack of honesty. Lack of ideas. Too many people. No agenda. No follow-through. Meetings that led to more meetings. Cook didn't quite know how to cure all these maladies. Maybe what Intuit needed was a leader more adept at motivating the troops, managing people, and running meetings in a more effective way.

To fill this position, Cook ended up recruiting Bill Campbell, a former college football coach turned tech exec, a man who later would be known as "the trillion-dollar coach," not only for his leadership at Intuit but for his mentorship of Steve Jobs and the Google cofounders Larry Page and Sergey Brin.

When Bill Campbell started as CEO in 1994, Scott Cook stepped back and remained chairman of the board as a new meetings culture at Intuit started to form. One could expect that Campbell would run Intuit as a series of half-time meetings, in which a great coach pivots the game plan and inspires the team to victory. After all, Campbell was a college player, then head coach of the Ivy League football team at Columbia University. The Campbell Trophy was already being given annually to the player who achieves excellence on the field, in academics, and in community service. But it was much more than motivational football-type speeches.

Cook attributes much of the success at Intuit to "the magic of Bill Campbell," and by that he mostly means the way he ran meetings and got the best out of individuals and teams. Drawn into the tech world by the challenge and the excitement of growing a startup, Campbell catapulted the company to a new level, with revenue growing 10 times in four years, to $800 million, and net profits reaching an incredible 50% of total sales. The growth came from expanding the Quicken franchise while also establishing TurboTax as the dominant way Americans would do their own taxes.

By 1999, this position in the market became even more valuable after Congress passed legislation to boost the number of e-filers from the current tiny fraction of Americans to 80% within the next few years. That meant Intuit had the chance to create the software that ensures seamless e-filing with the IRS. That led to more high-stakes meetings on how to get that done while also launching other new products.

My Opportunity to Join Intuit

It was at this time that I began to get a firsthand window into the meetings culture at Intuit. My startup, Boston Light Software, was caught in the frenzy of the dot-com boom. We were a small team that created websites for big companies and had just won a contract from *The Boston Globe* to create and help launch e-commerce on Boston.com. My old colleague Joe Mahoney from my first software job, at Interleaf, had a connection at Intuit and told me that they were looking to acquire dot-com companies. Joe asked whether I would want to help him prepare for and join a phone meeting with Intuit's acquisition team. In the meeting, I had the opportunity to chime in on evaluating and analyzing one of Intuit's acquisition targets—and to give them my recommendation whether to buy it or not. I recommended passing.

After the call, I heard from Joe that the Intuit team was so impressed with my analysis that they might be interested in acquiring my company. Pretty soon, I found myself in phone meetings with Intuit's lead negotiator, a super-tough woman named Kristen Brown, who cursed like a sailor and wasn't afraid of offending you. Brown offered me $2 million for my company. I declined, hung up, and walked away.

I met again with Joe, who pointed to the many outrageous dot-com deals that were happening. Yahoo! had just acquired the wildly overvalued GeoCities for $3.6 billion. Joe convinced me to go back and ask for $40 million. So that's what I did, surprising myself by even allowing myself to mention such a large number. This time, Kristen Brown cursed me out in two words, and she was the one who hung up on me.

Yet my cofounder, Karl Berry, and I ended up selling Boston Light in 1999 to Intuit for $33.5 million, which was beyond my imagination. The company itself wasn't worth anything close to that, but I was told that Intuit wanted me for my perspectives and qualities that I had put on display in phone calls. It occurred to me that I had become an instant millionaire due to a combination of luck—after the dot-com bubble burst a year later this wouldn't have happened—and my performance in meetings. With my Intuit stock alone worth $22 million, I decided to give away half of it to our 15 people, as a thank you and an incentive to join Intuit. They all agreed, and the entire team became full-time employees of this fast-growing outfit in Mountain View, California.

When Bill Campbell called to welcome me to Intuit, he told me that he was assigning most of my team to Intuit's budding QuickBooks franchise for small business owners. The number of meetings would be epic. My team developed a point of view of where to take QuickBooks—turning this stand-alone software package into a set of web-based services. I aimed to use our QSHOP e-commerce software to enable any enterprise to sell their goods and services on their own through QuickBooks. This way, it could become a much broader platform. But this could only happen if the decade-old software code underneath QuickBooks was replaced with modern software for the new era of the web.

This suggestion of a complete overhaul was resisted by the existing QuickBooks team, which set up a massive conflict that had to be worked out in a series of meetings. By the second meeting on the subject, the legacy QuickBooks team was clear: they were dead set against my proposed plan.

Plugging into the Meetings Culture at Intuit

I felt that I could prevail if I somehow got Bill Campbell on my side. The first time I met with him face-to-face, he made me feel like he woke up that day to see me. And while I was with him, probably just 25 minutes, he never looked at his watch. He didn't look at his BlackBerry. He just hyper-focused on me for 25 minutes. And when you meet someone who has the ability to listen so intently, it's chilling, like jumping into a cold lake, in that you are totally alert and present. Scott Cook has amazing meetings and listening skills as well. I'd give Scott a 9 out of 10. But the only people I'd give a 10 to would be Bill Campbell and Thích Nhất Hạnh, who once gave me the same chills when I encountered him in an audience at a Buddhism conference in Boston. In the Q&A, when an audience member asked for his wisdom, it felt like a private, intimate moment between that person and Nhất Hạnh that the rest of the audience was witnessing.

In case you don't know much about the Buddhist monk known as "the father of mindfulness," Nhất Hạnh engaged people by a practice he called *deep listening*.

"Listening is a very deep practice," said the Vietnamese peace activist who was once nominated for the Nobel Prize by Martin Luther King Jr. (Unlike King, he never did win it and seemed totally okay with that.) "You have to empty yourself," Nhất Hạnh continued. "You have to leave space in order to listen, especially to people we think are our enemies, the ones we believe are making our situation worse. When you have shown your capacity for listening and understanding, the other person will begin to listen to you." Campbell was this way, too.

My first meeting with Bill ended with not just a handshake but a hug. It was a demonstration of his magic powers. In this way, I felt that Bill was my champion, in that he was someone who could listen well and pay attention to me and make me feel heard. It's a remarkable feeling. But I was not alone in experiencing it. Everyone who left his office skipped down the hallway afterwards because he made them feel like a superhero. I've seen people come close to being like this, but I've never seen anyone crush it like Thích Nhất Hạnh and Bill Campbell. Both men have since passed on, but they will be remembered for these and other superpowers.

I aimed to take this deep listening skill into all my meetings at Intuit, most of which didn't include the CEO. My biggest immediate challenge was that meetings at Intuit headquarters in Silicon Valley were in a different location and time zone. I and most of my team lived in Boston and intended to stay there. When there was an important meeting on the schedule, my routine consisted of taking my daughter to school at 8 a.m., heading directly to Logan Airport, hopping on a flight to San Jose sometime after 9 a.m., and making it to Intuit soon after noon Pacific time.

As the new director of Intuit's small business internet efforts, I'd meet with engineers and managers there all afternoon. Often, I'd go out to dinner with one or more Intuit people, then hop on the red-eye, try to get some sleep on the plane, and land in Boston by 6 a.m., in time to take my daughter to school the next day. I did this once or twice per month. Occasionally, I'd stay over a night or camp out for a week.

As a natural-born workaholic, I learned a lot about work-life balance from the leader of the QuickBooks team, Craig Carlson. He was one of the most influential bosses of my career. Craig displayed incredible judgment, ran meetings incredibly well, hired well and fired well. But the amazing thing about Craig was his work-life balance. He played in an Ultimate Frisbee league that he led. Once, he was invited to a senior management meeting for Wednesday at 5 p.m. And Craig replied, "I can't go. I have an Ultimate Frisbee game." A top executive wanted to fire him just for that. Scott Cook intervened, and said, "No, you can't just fire Craig Carlson. He's our number one guy."

For all the times I couldn't attend meetings in person at Intuit, we convened on Webex, one of the early platforms for online video conferencing and team collaboration, a forerunner of Zoom. Wearing my headset for much of the day, I'd run some meetings and attend many others. Over hundreds of meetings, I developed a set of skills and guidelines that I deploy for online meetings to this day. One is to keep the energy level high. Get people excited to meet with the team and give them positive feedback. I reflected on the best meetings I've ever been in, which included Bill Campbell and Scott Cook, and I'd channel them.

If someone had a bright idea, I'd say that it's genius. For the person with the idea, it was the best day of the week for them. I'd give team members super positive feedback whenever they offered something smart or valuable. The key was to end the meeting not with a boring lull but on an energetic high as well.

I wasn't as good at giving negative feedback or delivering bad news. I learned how to do that from Craig Carlson. It's tough to do in general, but it's especially hard on a video call. Craig basically said, "You're doing a disservice to your people if you don't give them negative notes or outright criticism." So I would always say, "Hey, I want to give you some constructive feedback. And just to be clear, I'm not the perfect boss. I know that I have made a lot of mistakes, too, but it seems to me that you're doing X, Y, and Z." And I'd give feedback about what wasn't working well on the team. Whenever I had to fire someone on the California team, I would always fly out there to do it in person, not on video.

My overall goal was getting the QuickBooks package online as a service on the web. At the time, QuickBooks already dominated small business accounting, with about 80% market share. But it was an older and somewhat fragile system, with code about 10 years old. And what we were trying to do was open it up. I told Scott Cook that it's great that the company manages all this data for small business in America, but if they turn it into a web platform and have anyone in the world building small business apps that plug in, Intuit becomes a more powerful company. Scott became my co-cheerleader for the effort.

But it took me over a year of meetings to get the QuickBooks organization to fully buy-in and do this. They said it was impossible. The old code couldn't mesh with the new code. They said there will be security problems. I just kept at it, in meeting after meeting after meeting.

Confronting Conflict in Meetings

One of my allies was Hugh Molotsi, a staff software engineer who later rose to be an Intuit vice president over his 22-year career there. If a conflict arose in a meeting, one of my tendencies was to say, "Let's take this offline," and then I'd try to work it out one-on-one. Hugh said, "No, we should lean into the conflict with the group, not take it offline." Hugh went so far as to say, "We should look forward to meetings like we look forward to a movie. If there's no conflict, it's boring."

As it turned out, he was totally right, to the point where I came to enjoy fighting about stuff in meetings. If a topic became heated, and the team seemed dysfunctional, it was not a reason to run away from the conflict. After all, conflict is interesting. To me, this became a fundamental principle. Don't avoid conflict. Embrace it to the point when you promote the meeting with the conflict front and center. This became part of the meetings culture at Intuit, the idea that this will be a good meeting if we articulate our disagreements and resolve this conflict.

Hugh cites a memorable conflict in the QuickBooks Desktop development team. "We wanted to replace the QuickBooks Desktop database with a relational database that could scale to many more users," he recalls. "It was the engineering equivalent of open-heart surgery, and in early tests the initial performance wasn't good." The debate escalated to a senior-leadership off-site—one Hugh wasn't invited to.

At the off-site, the room voted to kill the new database. When I later heard about the decision, I made it clear I believed it was a mistake. Craig Carlson listened to my objection and—rather than brushing it aside—scheduled a follow-up so I could

make a fuller case to the broader team. In hindsight,
I should have come armed with more data, including
a few additional tests to bolster the argument. I made
my pitch, but when we went around the room,
I hadn't changed a single mind.

Hugh left dejected but glad he'd spoken up. Two days
later, new performance results arrived; a manager reversed his
view, the conversation reopened, and the decision changed.
The database was replaced—and QuickBooks Desktop still
runs on that relational database today.

The episode is a case study in leaning into conflict. Credit
goes to Craig for making space for a missing perspective and
for setting the expectation that, absent persuasion, the team
would align behind the decision.

"This was impactful," Hugh recalls. "In the end, it was a
good decision." Until then, Intuit had largely been a
consensus culture, and the downside is that difficult decisions
get put off or that dissenting opinions go unexpressed. But
when you argue and fight, it leads to more clarity over each
position. This is how conflict can lead to quicker and better
decisions.

The Bicoastal Meetings Man

My time at Intuit lasted until 2002, nearly four years. When
they had my "retirement" party, the enduring image that my
colleagues had of me was of me sitting in my Boston office in
my headset conducting bicoastal online meetings that were
scheduled for the California time zone. Some of the team
members made a custom "Mini-Me," an action figure that they
dressed just like me, in the shirt and jeans I usually wore, and
with my headset on. I don't know where they found a tiny
headset that fit a doll.

For much of my time at Intuit, the CEO was Steve Bennett, a former General Electric executive who grew up as the son of a football coach. Meanwhile, "Coach" Bill Campbell stepped into the role of chairman, and Scott Cook became chairman of the executive committee. "As a leadership trio, they are unique in Silicon Valley," wrote John Doerr, the legendary venture capitalist who backed Scott in the early years and remained on the board. "They provoke excellence, celebrate strategic thinking, inspire innovations, and obsess on serving customers."

Bennett changed one word in Intuit's values statement, from "think fast, move fast" to "think smart, move fast." His seven years as CEO were marked by explosive growth, with revenue tripling, from under $1 billion to nearly $3 billion, completing the transition of Intuit from startup to major corporation. I was there for the first part of that stretch, reaching a point where a quarter of US households were using at least one of Intuit's products.

I contributed by helping to open up QuickBooks to be a much broader, more useful, more powerful platform that could support outside apps, e-commerce, and a wider range of financial services. I led the creation of the Intuit Developer Network. We realized how much value that this brought to Intuit when Scott Cook and I joined the annual Dean Witter conference for tech investors. Scott Cook presented the vision for Intuit and handed off the QuickBooks portion to me. After our presentation, we were swamped with analyst meetings, and Bill Campbell texted me, "keep going, stock is up $17 a share!"

Meetings were a huge factor in that success, and as the team was sending me off, one of the nicest things said about me then was that I had changed the meetings culture at Intuit more than anyone in the company's history. "And you did it remotely," one executive noted. "How is that possible?"

First off, I did it by trying to be as high energy as possible. I realized that I was just a face on the screen. If I'm trying to change a culture that resisted transforming QuickBooks into a web platform for small business owners, I had to be as compelling as possible. That's why I learned how to sometimes be a little theatrical. I always tried to give everyone in the meeting a role to play. And that kept the energy moving around the virtual room.

I also liked to keep meetings small. Because if I was on video and I was talking to 10 people, it's really hard for a talking head up on the wall to influence 10 people. I tried to keep my meeting small to increase my influence. Three people. Three was my ideal number. I could influence three people. That was easy. Five was harder. Ten was really difficult. With 10 people, some start drifting off, checking their email, not actively participating. Ten people is okay for information sharing, but not for discussion.

When people in a meeting aren't paying full attention, they're quietly sucking energy out of the room, be it an actual room or a virtual one. Many meetings are about one person presenting a proposal and having the others review it and sometimes challenge it. But if you have 10 people challenging your idea, nothing can survive 10 critics. In the software industry, I've never seen something invented with 10 people in the room. It's best invented with two or three people.

If you want your idea to get through, make your meetings more cozy. Indeed, this became an enduring principle: keep meeting as small as you can. To this day, three people remains optimal for me. That's my sweet spot.

Yet it doesn't always make sense to keep meetings that small. We're going to dive into many types of meetings in this book. The situation suggests who gets invited. But the overriding principle is to keep meetings as small as possible.

Coined at Amazon.com, the two-pizza rule is the perfect rule of thumb that applies to teams that are focused on getting things done: *keep the number of people to those who can be served by two large pizzas.* That's anywhere from four people who are very hungry, and up to nine, if most people want just one or two slices.

Yet the two-pizza rule is not the biggest innovation in meeting culture to come out of Seattle, which leads us to Chapter 2, the story of what transpired at Amazon.com starting in 2004. It was an elevation of meetings culture that sent ripples through the business world when glimpses of this change were revealed outside the often-secretive company. At Intuit, for instance, Scott Cook started gathering as much information about what Jeff Bezos had done to change the nature of the business planning meeting. From media reports, from connecting with the company through emissaries and partnerships, "I became quite a fan of the way new business ideas were presented at Amazon," Scott says. "So, I just cloned the best parts of the Amazon ideas."

CHAPTER 2

How Amazon Revolutionized Presentations

In early 2004, Jeff Bezos and his "shadow" executive Colin Bryar were flying across the country in the days before onboard Wi-Fi. Sitting side by side, they were using the time to discuss new ways to address a drawback with meetings at Amazon, especially among the S-Team, the senior leadership roster of Amazon.com's top executives. This business planning team met once per week for up to four hours, and each of the leaders was now being asked to present visions for the company's future. That meant the inevitable series of PowerPoint presentations in which execs would "walk" the team through a series of slides consisting of bullet-point lists. Sometimes, there would be a question on a slide that required a deep-dive discussion, but the presenter would say, "let's put a pin in that," and hold off the question because it would be "addressed on a later slide."

As the CEO's shadow, it was central to Colin's job to make meetings with Bezos as productive as possible, and he was worried that the current format wouldn't work well for their next series of challenges. The 10th anniversary of the company was approaching, marking when Bezos wrote the business plan for Amazon.com on a road trip from New York City to Seattle. A decade later, the company was now at a crossroads. During its first era, Amazon had grown by expanding categories of online retail, moving beyond books into selling almost everything. That took Amazon past $5 billion in annual revenue, but in most quarters the company posted either razor-slim profits or lost money.

New ideas on how to drive growth and profits were floating around the company. Capitalize on the shift from print books, music CDs, and movie DVDs to online digital content. Launch an annual subscription service that covers shipping charges. Develop hardware such as smart speakers and handheld book readers. Start selling its home-grown web services software to outside companies. All these concepts were far more complex than anything the company had ever done. Moving into entirely new businesses or embracing new business models requires a higher density of information coupled with ironclad logic for strategy and execution.

For the plane ride, Colin had brought a copy of *The Visual Display of Quantitative Information*, the classic 1983 book on presenting data by Edward Tufte, a statistics professor at Yale University. He also brought the 2003 follow-up booklet, "The Cognitive Style of PowerPoint: Why Pitching Out Corrupts Within," in which Tufte argues in 23 pages that most slideshow presentations are beset with crippling and pernicious drawbacks. When advancing from slide to slide, it's difficult to refer one idea to another. Bullet-point lists are abbreviated and don't enable a full expression of an idea. The visual effects are often more distracting than enlightening. PowerPoint is supposed to make things clear and simple, but it strips arguments of context and nuance.

According to Colin, this was the sentence that sold Jeff on the idea of making a momentous change in Amazon's meeting culture: "As analysis becomes more causal, multivariate, comparative, evidence-based, and resolution intensive, the more damaging the bullet list becomes." Tufte was emphatic on his recommendation: "From now on, your presentation software is Microsoft Word, not PowerPoint. Get used to it."

On June 9, 2004, all senior leaders at Amazon received an email entitled, "No PowerPoint presentations from now on at S-Team." It was sent by Colin but was clearly sanctioned by Jeff. Pitch decks from laptops were to be replaced by paper handouts.

Written in Word, these multipage memos were to be called *Narratives*. There were many reasons for the change. Ideas, not presenters, matter the most. Some people were more charming and better than others at public speaking. Charm should be irrelevant. It was the information, the argument, and the story that should win the day.

Information density was key. Up to 4,000 characters in 11-point type could fit on a printed single-spaced page. That compares to just 440 characters on a typical PowerPoint slide that had to be read from a distance. That's about 9× more information per presentation. Colin coined a new term: *the Narrative Information Multiplier.* It was a way to get far more information flowing through the S-Team. As a rule of thumb, people can read written material faster than people can speak it. Logic can flow in a tighter way in a written narrative, whereas a set of slides can be riddled with plot holes, flaws in thinking that could doom a new initiative.

The backlash from the S-Team was swift and nearly universal. Nobody seemed to like the idea. They were comfortable creating slide decks, and no one knew how to write one of these narratives. Those with presentations set for the next two weeks went into panic mode. Colin scrambled to train everyone on the new method and offered examples of effective narratives. Bezos raised the bar in a follow-up email, slamming PowerPoint for giving presenters "permission to gloss over ideas, flatten out any sense of relative importance, and ignore the interconnectedness of ideas." He argued that "the narrative structure of a good memo forces better thought and better understanding of what's more important than what, and how things are related."

When some of the first narrative memos were handed out at S-Team meetings, they tended to go too long, with one rambling on for 40 pages. This resulted in the six-page limit. Since it took an average of three minutes to read each page, everyone could finish within 20 minutes. That meant that when a narrative was presented at a one-hour S-Team meeting, the first third would be reserved for everyone sitting in silence reading. Since no one was expected to review the document ahead of time, no one had to lie and say they'd read the memo. This way, it was fresh in everyone's minds, and they could make notes and come up with questions as they read. No stage presence, no personal charm—just the idea presented in a compelling flow of words.

Over time, these "six-pagers" came to be written in a common nine-part format:

1. The Introduction of the proposed idea, business, product, or concept
2. The Tenets—the underlying truths that stick close to the company's core principles, such as customer obsession, starting with the optimal customer experience and working backwards to deliver that experience
3. Accomplishments that have been achieved thus far
4. Misses, or mistakes that team members can learn from
5. Proposals for next period, such as next steps or follow-up initiatives
6. Headcount—estimates of how many employees would be required
7. P&L—estimates on revenue and profits
8. An FAQ section that poses and answers anticipated questions
9. An optional Appendix, including tables, charts, and backup data that isn't counted as part of the six pages

If it's a 30-minute meeting, then the Narrative should be three pages, sticking to the guideline that the first third of the meeting is spent reading and pondering the memo in silence. During the meeting, the presenter could elaborate on certain points, but should not "walk people through the document," as that would be redundant. After all, they just read it. Indeed, most of the rest of the meeting was reserved for Q&A and discussion.

Those who posed a strong or insightful question could end up in a discussion in which they were shaping a new idea. That could result in becoming a key team member for a new initiative. But getting an instant green light was rare. Jeff was known to read these narratives with complete focus and concentration and be among the last to finish reading. According to Colin, he'd usually arrive at original insights that no one else thought of. When pressed on how he did this, Jeff would say that he assumes every sentence is wrong until proven otherwise. This emphasis on critical thinking caused everyone else to improve the quality of their thinking as expressed in the document. Typically, it would take days to write a solid narrative before printing out copies and bringing it to a high-stakes meeting.

Making Narratives the Centerpiece of Meetings

The decisions that Amazon made after embracing narrative-driven meetings were not always rewarded by the marketplace. Not many people remember Amazon's foray into phones. Creating and launching the Fire Phone, which sported a unique 3-D display, represented a major investment of time and money. In meetings, the narrative was convincing that Amazon must make devices. But once it was launched, it seemed that no one wanted the Fire Phone, and it was pulled from the market in less than a year.

As Bezos justified it, this was the inevitable result of being committed to invention, that it has always been a key tenet at Amazon that if you are not failing some of the time, you're not inventing. Asked by a reporter to explain the Fire Phone flop, Bezos laughed. "If you think that's a big failure, we're working on much bigger failures right now—and I am not kidding."

Much of the pressure on presenting new initiatives fell on an executive named Bill Carr, who had joined the company in 1999 when Amazon was still in a single building on Second Avenue in Seattle, when Jeff's desk was a discarded door resting on file cabinets. As director of digital media, it was Carr's job to write narratives for meetings that asked and answered questions such as these:

> Should we acquire companies to accelerate our entry into digital?
> Should we focus on books, music, or video?
> Should we build a subscription service?
> Should we make it free, with ads, let people buy à la carte, or all of the above?
> Should we build our own devices or partner with manufacturers?
> What capabilities do we need to build for digital that we don't have now?

As Amazon contemplated its foray into digital music, Bill, Jeff, and a newly promoted vice president of digital media, Steve Kessel, paid a visit to Apple headquarters in Cupertino for a meeting hosted by Steve Jobs. The iPod was taking off in remarkable fashion, Jobs reported, and the business model of charging 99 cents per song was being embraced by the market. Jobs also had a few words of warning: that Amazon's sales of music CDs would disappear sooner than they thought.

Jobs then showed a demo of a new program of which he was especially proud, iTunes for Windows. This meant Apple was expanding its music franchise beyond Macs, which was only 10% of the market, to the much wider PC user base. For the team at Amazon, the biggest takeaway was to steer clear of competing directly against Apple in music. Most of all, Amazon should not make its own music device.

This decision seems obvious now, but it was not quite so at Microsoft, which decided to launch its Zune music device in direct competition with Apple. The PowerPoint slides that presented Zune to the senior leadership at Microsoft may have seemed jazzy at the time, but they must have also masked major flaws in the argument to move forward with it. Featuring software riddled with bugs and a design that couldn't hold a candle to the iPod, the Zune turned into a spectacular flop, a massive waste of time and money, an instant laughingstock of both the tech world and the music world.

At Amazon, the approach to digital consumed six months of research into the new media landscape that was presented in weekly S-Team meetings run by Jeff. By the time 2004 was over, the team had made a big decision: the focus should be on e-books and that Amazon should make its own reading device. Asked in the presence of Amazon's chief financial officer how much investment he was willing to plow into the creation and launch of what became the Kindle platform, Bezos turned to the CFO and laughed once again, "How much money do we got?"

Much of the impetus for the decision was presented in weekly meetings. Carr and Kessel delivered dense narratives, sending the S-Team into deep dives on what Amazon had become, what its capabilities were, what skills it lacked, and what its role was in the publishing and bookselling ecosystem, which was a continued subject of controversy in that industry.

In the end, the argument that Amazon should go all-in on designing and making a reading device and launching a new business model for e-books won the day. Yet the decision was far from unanimous. Carr had argued that Amazon had no business getting into making hardware, that it was too capital intensive, and that it violated Amazon's frugality principle that stated investments in new products should happen gradually.

Yet Kessel argued that it was precisely Amazon's role to be at the center of a new e-books ecosystem, in the way that Apple's iTunes was now at the center of digital music. Jeff went with Kessel, who became known as the man behind Kindle.

Looking back, from the vantage point of Kindle's first decade in the market, Kessel admitted that he was wrong about many of the details, even though he was right about the overall argument that he propounded in a series of narrative-driven meetings. "Originally," he said, "I told Jeff it would take us about 18 months to build the Kindle and we could do it with a couple handfuls of folks. It took us three-and-a-half years and a lot more than a couple of handfuls of folks."

Some meetings focused on Kessel narratives that seemed outlandish at the time, most notably presenting the concept that the Kindle device should have something known as Whispernet, a built-in chip that connected over cellular, so that readers could purchase and download a new e-book while relaxing at the beach or by the pool. Also this: forgo the backlit screens that are on the market and develop a new screen based on the E-Ink project at the MIT Media Lab that was optimized for presenting black-and-white text only—no colors, no graphics—and could adjust lighting levels depending on whether it was outdoor or indoor reading. At the time, these ideas might have seemed insane, but they were backed up by precisely written narratives that contained more information than was possible to present in a short PowerPoint deck.

As it turned out, these features are what made the Kindle device a hit. And yet there was even more to it. Amazon's meetings with all the major publishers resulted in an industry-wide convergence on $9.99 being the standard price point for an e-book. In 2007, the Kindle platform launched with 90,000 e-book titles available on day one, versus just 20,000 on the competing Sony e-reader.

All those information-dense meetings paid off. By 2008, the Kindle device was selling as fast as Amazon could make them, and publishers moved to make a Kindle edition standard for all new titles. When Oprah, known as "the Queen of Reading," devoted an entire show to the Kindle and proclaimed, "It's absolutely my new favorite thing in the world," Kindle's staying power was assured. The meeting culture at Amazon was clearly a huge factor in this success.

When Meetings Turn Urgent

In mid-October 2004, Jeff presented a narrative to the S-Team previewed in an email: "We should not be satisfied with the growth of our retail business. This is a house-on-fire issue, and we need to dramatically improve the customer experience around shopping. We need a shipping membership program. Let's build and launch it by the end of the year."

Going into the holiday shopping season, other retailers were focused on executing their strategies, not creating new ones. To some members of the S-Team, Jeff's email seemed impetuous, a false crisis, a fire drill that came at the worst time, because it could distract a company from staying on course as Christmas approached.

A divide opened on the S-Team and debate spilled into meetings. Most members fell into the "stay the course" camp, arguing that Amazon's retail revenue last year increased by

29%, a healthy clip. They suggested incremental tweaking to shipping and fulfillment operations and to continue the successful Super Saving Shipping, which enabled customers to increase their order to $49 to activate free shipping on most items. That was lowered to $25 for certain items.

Yet there remained a trade-off, as items shipping for free often took additional days to avoid losing money on the order. Bezos wasn't having it. It was true, he argued, that Amazon was growing and had become the online retail leader. But less than 2% of US retail sales were online. Amazon was only nailing two out of three key metrics—selection and price—but failing on convenience, he argued. Research showed that many customers balked at shipping costs. The choice should not be "slow and free" versus "fast and expensive." Rather, Amazon needed to move toward "fast and free."

A narrative memo on the shipping issue came from an unlikely place. A software engineer named Charlie Ward who worked on the code to implement Super Saver Shipping had an idea: "Why couldn't we have customers pay an annual subscription fee that would include free shipping for a year?" Kim Rachmeler, who ran customer service, believed this would be a big win for customers and encouraged him to circulate the memo. "You may have something there, Charlie." Ward fired off his short narrative before heading off on a planned vacation to Italy. When he returned, he heard about the urgent email from Jeff Bezos and how Amazon was now answering his exact question.

The project was code-named "Futurama" because shipping unlimited goods for free within a day or two seemed like science fiction at the time. Approaching the holidays, development and logistics teams scrambled to create what became Amazon Prime. It took so much focus from Bezos and the senior team that they had to delay the quarterly earnings announcement from January to the planned launch date, February 2, 2005. That's when the world learned of the initial $79 annual subscription. Customers took to it immediately, and one media report concluded that "Amazon single-handedly—and permanently—raised the bar for convenience in online shopping."

Amazon's meeting culture enabled one of the biggest innovations in the history of retail to go from idea to rollout in four months. Amazon Prime grew so popular that it surpassed 100 million subscribers by 2018, representing about 75% of US households. That's an astonishing number. It makes Prime one of the prime reasons Amazon dominates an online marketplace that now accounts for more than 20% of the total $7 trillion US retail economy. Yet there were several additional major narratives that were playing out in Amazon's meeting culture at the same time.

Learning from Failure in Meetings

A strategy for online video became one of the biggest conundrums debated among Amazon's S-Team. Amazon was doing brisk business selling DVDs, competing with the DVD-by-mail subscription business pioneered by Netflix. But in 2004, the opportunity to serve movies on demand via the internet appeared on the horizon. Bezos charged Bill Carr with coming up with a customer-focused solution.

Carr convened a series of meetings. The earliest meetings focused on figuring out how consumers could best download movies and TV shows from Amazon's online store for viewing on laptops. Narratives were presented on how to price movies for rental and ownership, how to negotiate obtaining titles from the Hollywood studios, how to manage digital rights to prevent piracy, and how to let customers store movies they purchased. Eventually, there were meetings on whether to launch special hardware devices, and meetings on how to allocate capital to launch this new video business.

The first iteration, Amazon Unbox, was unveiled in 2006 and offered 5,000 movies and TV shows. It was an "outright failure," according to Carr. Customers were frustrated with download speeds. Sometimes, a download would hang up, freeze their computer, require a reboot, forcing the customer to try again or give up. Video on laptops sometimes skipped or stopped. The team planned to create a special DVD burner, so that customers could download movies onto discs to be popped into DVD players. Yet that idea was abandoned as a temporary, bad stopgap solution.

Just a few days after the launch of Unbox, Bezos called Carr and other video team members into an emergency meeting in his office. The CEO was disappointed by all the customer complaints and angry that the team had launched such a sub-par service. Carr thought he was about to get fired and braced himself for losing his job. "Why would I fire you now?" Bezos said. "I just made a million-dollar investment in you. Figure out and clearly document where you went wrong. Share what you've learned with other leaders."

A series of meetings focused on comparing Amazon's failures to an upstart service called YouTube, which seemed to prove that video quality didn't matter much. Consumers loved watching cat videos and silly pranks as long as it was easy and free of glitches. Google bought the startup for $1.65 billion. At the same time, Apple was now selling movies and shows on iTunes that could be watched on a laptop or even an iPod. A new device, AppleTV, made it easy to stream films and shows on televisions. By early 2007, Netflix launched its first video streaming service, called Watch Now, and was offering it free to its DVD-by-mail subscribers. By October, a studio-backed service called Hulu was offering an ad-supported service that let you watch some of the biggest TV shows for free. Amazon decided to partner with TiVo, which had a hot-selling box that could serve movies and shows to television sets.

Amazon's meetings about video continued over six years of failure after failure as competitors were gaining traction. The S-Team reached a conclusion: its strategy of only being the middleman, serving other people's content to other people's devices, was the fundamental flaw. Multipage narratives read in silence at the outset of meetings presented concepts for new devices: the Fire TV, the Kindle Fire Tablet, the Fire Stick, and the Echo speaker controlled by the Alexa natural language interface. Investments were piling up, yet after a half dozen video meetings in 2010, it was still the case that Amazon was getting nowhere toward becoming a leading player in streaming or selling video on demand.

That's when Bezos presented a simple idea: "let's make video free for Prime members." It was the meeting that broke the spell. By 2011, millions of Prime Video users were taking advantage of their free new benefit. Yet the biggest set of decisions hinged on whether to invest in creating original content. By 2013, just as Netflix had premiered *House of Cards*, its first original series, the new Amazon Studios was operating out of offices in Santa Monica, where a team of freshly hired development executives were producing original films and TV shows.

These meetings were all about whether to greenlight scripts, movie pitches, or series concepts. Only when shows such as *Transparent, Mozart in the Jungle*, and *The Man in the High Castle* became Emmy-winning hits did 10 years of meetings on what to do about video finally pay off. Amazon had now emerged as one of the major players in the most legendary locale for meetings, Hollywood.

Probably the Smartest Thing We Ever Did

Meetings that centered around debating six-page narratives became the secret weapon that Amazon deployed across all its lines of business. But one highly secretive new venture had financial impact that would surpass Kindle, Prime Video, Amazon Studios, and even Amazon Prime itself. Running in parallel with the launch of all those new global brands, this series of meetings would take Amazon way beyond its core business. Of course, we're talking about Amazon Web Services, or AWS, a separately managed business unit led by Andy Jassy, who started as Jeff's shadow in Amazon's early days. Jassy would launch and grow the franchise that would deliver explosive revenue growth and the lion's share of the company's profits.

The meetings that led to the launch and expansion of AWS were the company's most secretive. Back in 2004, Amazon made almost all its revenue sourcing, selling, and delivering physical products. Its move into digital media meant it was now also sourcing, selling, and delivering goods over the internet onto devices and screens. But this new business in cloud computing was something else entirely. It meant being put into direct competition with tech titans such as Google and its Seattle neighbor, Microsoft. That meant all details and trade secrets had to be kept under wraps. But it also meant that Amazon's secret weapon, its unique meeting culture, also had to be kept secret, and it remained largely unknown outside the company for years.

Only in 2018, when Amazon's market value had surpassed $1 trillion and Jeff Bezos had become known as the richest man in the world did this competitive edge get revealed to outsiders in a big way. "Many, many years ago, we outlawed PowerPoint presentations at Amazon," Bezos said at the Bush Center's Forum on Leadership. "It totally revolutionized the way we do meetings at Amazon," he added. "And it's probably the smartest thing we ever did."

A video of Jeff's talk about meetings went viral, and the business press made it seem like this was his secret to success. A typical headline: "Why Jeff Bezos Makes Amazon Execs Read 6-Page Memos at the Start of Each Meeting." Suddenly, all kinds of companies were contemplating starting meetings with each attendee sitting and silently reading a six-page, narratively structured memo for the first 20 minutes.

The reason that everyone must read it at the same time, Bezos explained, is to prevent executives from "bluffing their way through the meeting as if they've read the memo." Yet the core of the meeting itself takes place after the reading, during which executives are encouraged to make notes. "It's supposed to create the context for what will then be a good discussion," Bezos said.

But creating the narrative itself isn't easy. "The great narratives are written and rewritten, shared with colleagues who are asked to improve the work, set aside for a couple of days, and then edited again with a fresh mind," he said. "They simply can't be done in a day or two. It's harder for the author, but it forces the author to clarify their own thinking."

My former colleagues at Intuit and I knew about Amazon's meeting culture much earlier only because Scott Cook made it part of his mission to get inside Amazon to find out how to clone it. Yet even though many business leaders began adapting one of Amazon's biggest competitive advantages to their own companies, it wasn't the be-all-and-end-all solution to having better meetings. There were still even bigger barriers standing in the way of forging a more effective meeting culture in corporate America.

CHAPTER 3

How Constant Contact and OpenTable Confronted Gender Bias

In spring 2007, Gail Goodman was busy holding a "bake-off," a series of meetings in which her company, Constant Contact, would choose which investment bank would take her company public in the fall. As chairperson and CEO, it was up to her and the board to select the firm to win the lucrative contract. Gail was a mentor for me in the early part of my career, so I know her as a strong leader who is ultra-effective in meetings. She tells you the truth, even if it's something you didn't want to hear. A veteran of several successful startups, by that point Gail had led Constant Contact into the top spot in the market for web services that helped companies create customized email lists for outbound messaging and growing sales.

Next up to make its pitch for the initial public offering (IPO) bake-off: a top New York investment bank. The meeting day arrived, and a team of investment bankers from this major financial institution streamed into Constant Contact's boardroom in Boston. "We had been working with the bank's Boston team," Goodman recalls. "They brought in the senior guy from New York because they wanted to show that they really wanted to win this."

But then a disturbing thing kept happening. "He never made eye contact with me, and he kept interrupting me," Gail recalls. "It was insane." Other board members picked up on it right away, looking around the room as if something surreal was happening.

Running though Gail's mind were these questions: *Did he not read the briefing? Does he not know I'm the CEO and the board chair? Or worse, does he know and not care?*

The irony was off the charts, as the business of Constant Contact was all about making sales and marketing more targeted, precise, and effective, and this senior finance leader didn't seem to know that he was alienating the most important decision-maker in the room. The men from the bank were quick to interject their own points, but they followed the senior guy's lead addressing only the men on the board, without looking at Gail or talking to her directly.

As a result, the pitch went horribly. "Afterwards," says Gail, "my board at least was horrified enough to say, 'They're off the list.'" The big New York bank had disqualified itself by exhibiting a most extreme case of gender bias in a high-stakes meeting. Goodman and her board instead chose other bankers to stage the IPO on the Nasdaq, which went extremely well, as the first market price for the newly issued stock exceeded the expected range.

Goodman tells this story not to embarrass anyone, only as an extreme example of what she has seen as common in the tech industry and in finance. "Men interrupt and talk over women all the time," she says. "Men have some kind of zone-out filter where women are talking and then they say the same thing the woman said. They're not doing it because they're mocking the woman. They literally weren't listening when the woman was talking."

"It's crazy," Gail continues. "I think it is less so in the younger generation, but it certainly was true in my generation." The gender bias can extend to many different aspects of a meeting. For instance, Gail adds, "It's harder for women to have strongly held opinions and not be seen as strident. A man can get so sure of themselves and slam his fists on the table. If a woman does that, she's losing her cool or being emotional."

How does one deal with that? "Take deep breaths," says Gail.

In other words, men who practice gender bias in meetings, whether inadvertently or not, are ultimately only hurting themselves as well as their companies. The investment banker from New York lost the deal, after all. You never want to piss off someone like Gail Goodman or any woman who is part of your team. Yet it's not up to women to fix this pervasive situation. Men must become aware whenever they or some other guy interrupts women, talks over them, ignores them, or takes credit for their ideas.

If you want to create a strong meeting culture at your organization, you must call out this behavior. Typically, it's best to do so after the meeting, in a side conversation. This way, it's not by way of embarrassing someone, by catching them in the act, but rather by enabling some self-reflection before the next meeting takes place. While it's not easy to root out, and it might take repeated conversations, this is the best way to overcome gender bias that is harming meeting culture and holding back companies from achieving more.

The payoff of doing so is real. Powerful women like Gail Goodman have championed my work. And I have always tried to pay it forward. Which brings me to the remarkable story of a woman whom I once hired at Kayak.

When the Tables Are Turned

In 2010, Debby Soo was an MBA student at MIT's Sloan School of Business when I hired her as a summer intern at Kayak. I was impressed by her story of growing up in San Francisco as the only child of parents who emigrated from Taiwan and set up an old school travel agency, where every reservation was handled with care. At first, her folks operated the agency out of Debby's bedroom while she was at school. After school, she helped them finish up their work, so she could finally get them out of there. I thought that was a great background for joining our team at Kayak, where we aimed to create the world's most productive travel search company.

After graduating from Stanford and working in investment banking, Debby decided she wanted to become an operator of a company, not an advisor to one. She joined Google and distinguished herself there before heading to MIT and now Kayak, where her internship turned into a 10-year run. "Kayak became a real bootcamp for me," Debby recalls. She worked across product, marketing, sales, and business development, spending most of those years building Kayak's international presence.

She launched Kayak in Brazil and became the general manager of our Asia-Pacific business.

In meetings, Debby was direct and transparent, some would say blunt. But it was all in an effort to learn from people and distill takeaway lessons from both success and failure. "I tried to be of the mindset that every experience, good and bad, was a learning opportunity," she says. "I always tell my teams that I know I've succeeded as a manager and leader if I'm *not* the smartest person in the room with all the answers."

By the time Priceline (now Booking.com) acquired Kayak for about $2 billion in 2012, Debby was one of our most valuable people, mastering our meeting culture and developing a candid style of managing others. "People generally know where they stand with me, and I really appreciate it when I know where I stand with them," she says. "To be direct and transparent, there needs to be a lot of trust—trust between people and trust between different teams. When there is a strong sense of trust in a company and people feel safe psychologically to make mistakes and take risks, magical things can happen."

Debby enabled magical things not only at Kayak but also at our new sister company OpenTable, a website and app for restaurant reservations. Priceline/Booking acquired it for

$2.6 billion in 2014 yet left it to be independently run, just as Kayak remains. Eight years later, at the depth of the COVID pandemic, when restaurant reservations barely existed anymore, Debby Soo was named the new CEO of OpenTable.

She appointed two other Asian American women who launched their careers at Kayak to her leadership trio: Amy Wei became chief operating officer, and Susan Lee became chief strategy officer. Debby and her team led OpenTable through its darkest times during COVID. And after dining-in restaurants came back, they built it into a market-dominating company that now helps fill tables for more than a billion meals per year at 60,000 restaurants in 80 countries.

If you would think that men would be self-aware enough to be on their best behavior in meetings with Debby, Amy, and Susan, you would be wrong. Asked if she has been in more than one meeting in which a man interrupted a woman, a man ignored a woman, or a man took credit for a woman's ideas, Debby replied, "Yes! Yes! Yes!"

"Some men tune out when a woman is talking in a meeting," she continued. "I see it all the time. They don't seem to realize they're doing it. It's an interesting dynamic. Since I'm the CEO, men don't often interrupt me. But men interrupt Amy, my number two, all the time, right in front of me."

This doesn't happen as frequently at OpenTable, she clarified, because it's not tolerated. But it happens much more frequently with outside meetings with business partners or with the parent company. During regularly scheduled Zoom meetings, "I always spot one male executive looking out the window whenever a woman is talking. A woman makes a point, is ignored, and a man makes the same point later, attempting to get credit for it. This happens all the time."

I told you Debby was blunt. Yet it's not her job to call it out while it's happening. It's up to men in leadership positions to become more self-aware, to learn how to shut up until a woman is finished making her point, to give credit where credit is due, and to champion women who show themselves to be exceptionally capable.

The way Debby puts it, this lack of self-awareness puts some men at a disadvantage. "Meanwhile," she adds, "women have a lot of advantages. We often have a more holistic view of what we are discussing. The women on my team are more creative in problem-solving. Women do the balancing act of life way more frequently than men. The three of us are all moms of young kids. It's a high cognitive load to take on."

In other words, guys, you really need to get this right. If you want to be invited to important meetings more often instead of less often, you've got to get with the program, especially because meetings are happening all the time, not just at the office and on video calls.

When Meeting Culture Meets Restaurant Culture

Indeed, Debby Soo has extended her leadership style from the Zoom screen to the boardroom to restaurants all over the world. "I love having meetings at restaurants," she says. "There's a kind of intimacy that comes with dining with someone else. It's a deeper connection to the person."

Due to her position leading OpenTable, these opportunities arise every week. She's become especially sharp about delivering her insights about meetings at bars and restaurants, where people often behave differently than they do in conference rooms or on Zoom. "You get to see how a colleague or a potential business partner treats the server, which is sometimes not graciously. Some men treat waitstaff as invisible. But we have stories of both men and women who are demeaning to the waitstaff. Women can sometimes be overly prescriptive and condescending. I recall a time when a woman had 15 alterations to her order."

A meeting over a meal provides "a wonderful window into the whole person," she adds. Spending time this way is especially valuable for evaluating a partnership. Debby tells of a situation where OpenTable was looking to form a partnership with a tech company. It was between Company A and Company B. The CEO of Company A invited Debby, Amy, and Susan to their offices in the Bay Area, and that meeting went fine.

But Company B was headquartered in New York, and the CEO wanted to meet with the OpenTable team in San Francisco. "We made a dinner reservation," Debby recalls. "And getting to know each was a different vibe. We in the hospitality business need to understand hospitality. Having a meal together enables you to see what drives people. We chose Company B."

"When it comes to the decision by a restaurant to consider joining OpenTable, it always centers [on] experiencing the restaurant. Most restaurant owners will ask, 'Have you dined with us?' They want us to meet them in their restaurant. It's less about the meeting itself than being a guest in their environment. We like to show up frequently, meet new people, and share a meal. This has added up to years of our people going to dinners and happy hours, and meeting the staff and the chefs."

There's the story of Angie Mar, a late-blooming real estate rep from Seattle who metamorphosed into a celebrity chef specializing in French cuisine at New York City's Beatrice Inn. According to a review on Eyeswoon, "Angie undoubtedly did what she set out to do in making The Beatrice into a restaurant that celebrates family and history. There we can feel at home as we devour Angie's dishes. With just five to six components per plate, she describes her food as restrained and like music, celebrating high and low notes, masculine and feminine influences."

Yet sometime before the pandemic, Angie's restaurant dropped OpenTable and went with a different reservation platform. Several months after becoming CEO, when COVID was finally subsiding, Debby Soo made a point of heading to New York and dining at Angie's new restaurant, Le B, to get a chance to be across the table from her.

Debby brought her three-year-old son, who doesn't do French cuisine. "Angie went out of her way to personally prepare noodles for him," Debby recalled. A great connection was made.

"Are you ready to come back?" Debby asked her.

Angie didn't answer either way, saying she needs time to think about it. Six months afterwards, Le B returned to OpenTable. "What happens when people meet this way matters to my customer base," Debby concludes. "There are some things that AI can never replace."

Driver, Approver, Consulted, Informed

Meanwhile, back at the office, OpenTable under Debby Soo adopted a meetings framework designed to improve a team's effectiveness and velocity on projects by assigning team members roles and responsibilities for making decisions. The model has become known as DACI for Driver (the person who drives the decision), Approver (the person who approves the decision), Contributors (the people who support and help the project), and Informed (the people who need to be kept in the loop).

Amazingly, the model was developed at Intuit by Scott Cook and his legendary leadership team. To me, this shows how meeting culture has followed a progression, where best practices from one company have spread to more and more over time. Not every innovation in better meetings needs to be adopted by everyone. For instance, OpenTable has only partially moved to the Amazon model of written documents instead of decks for presenting new ideas and concepts.

But Debby saw the DACI model as a way of bringing discipline to a meeting culture that was on the verge of dysfunction. "When I became CEO of OpenTable in 2020, we had meetings with 150 people," she recalls. "Large groups would go to stand-up meetings, where updates would be presented. They were mostly one-way info sessions. They weren't engaging for most people. No decisions were made."

The new CEO developed what she describes as "a strong opinion" about these meetings. "People came to meetings to be seen rather than have an important impact. If you weren't a stakeholder in the meeting topic, I said, you shouldn't be there. It's only important for you to be there if you have something to contribute."

That's how meetings came to be run at OpenTable: by keeping the list of invitees tight. Sometimes it's just drivers and approvers, sometimes select contributors are invited. Those who need to be informed can learn about it afterwards by receiving a meeting summary or a recording. As you'd expect by now, Debby is blunt about the need to cut people out of meetings. "People who fall off the invite list get hurt when they find out they're not going to a big meeting," she says. "But we aim to be transparent by providing access to the meeting later through a recording."

Indeed, the recordings are valuable for other reasons, too. When it comes to those who are informed, at OpenTable this extends to new employees who are trying to get up to speed about how things work. "Culturally," Debby says, "this is how we train new people: by having them listen to important meetings."

What the DACI model does is establish critical ground rules for a good meeting: Who holds decision rights? Who owns the risk of a move here? You want to be clear about what you want to come out of the meeting. Afterwards, you want to know answers to these questions: What have we accomplished? What are the action items from the meeting? Those action items are the most important part of the meeting summary sent to all the DACI members via email. Anyone can come up with an idea for continuing whatever is still open to discussion.

When it comes to models and frameworks for meetings, I fancy myself a connoisseur. I appreciate how DACI is an adaptation of RACI (Responsible, Accountable, Consulted, Informed), an earlier model that the leaders at Intuit refined and greatly improved. The clear, action-oriented Driver is much more effective than the vague, passive-sounding term, Responsible. The Approver is also an active term, whereas Accountable sounds like some people are bound to receive the blame. The term Contributors invokes collaboration, whereas Consulted sounds like those are the people who we can easily ignore. Informed is the one term that remains the same.

And so, in geeking out about meeting models, we are arriving at the part of the book that I would call "the true confessions of a meeting maniac." It centers on the story of how we founded Kayak and grew it into the most productive and profitable company in the online travel industry.

CHAPTER 4

How Kayak Became Maniacal About Meetings

It became known as my billion-dollar meeting. After leaving Intuit in 2003, I was invited to become an entrepreneur-in-residence at General Catalyst, a major venture capital firm based in Harvard Square by the bustling Charles Hotel, a hot spot for high-powered breakfast, lunch, and dinner meetings. One day, as I'm leaving the office, one of the partners sees me and asks what I'm up to, and I tell him I'm evaluating a mobile gaming company for them. He says, "I have a guy here named Steve Hafner, one of the founders of the Orbitz travel site, and he wants to create a travel search engine. Will you meet with him?" I say that I'm happy to.

After we were introduced, Steve and I took the elevator downstairs to the building's ground floor restaurant, Legal Seafoods. We had a couple of gin and tonics, kind of a liquid lunch, and Steve pitched me the concept for Kayak. (That wasn't the name for the company yet.) Steve told me about how travel and tourism is 8% of the US economy and is the biggest segment in e-commerce. There needed to be a search engine built and optimized for travel but doesn't do any transactions. Instead, it would make money on referral fees to the major reservation sites. A Google for travel. I loved the idea. I told Steve that I thought it was exciting. Here's how our deal went down:

> Steve says, "I'm looking for a chief technology officer."
> I say, "I'll find one for you. How much will you pay?"
> And he says, "$150,000 a year and 4% of the company."
> I say, "That sounds great. I bet I can find you some good candidates."
> He says, "Why don't you do it?"
> And I say, "No, I'm going to create another startup."
> And Steve says, "What would it take for you to do it?"
> I say, "At a minimum, 50% of the company."
> He puts his hand across the table. He says, "Done."

We shook hands. And just like that, 45 minutes after meeting Steve, we agreed to be equal cofounders.

A decade later, Kayak was acquired by Priceline.com (now Booking.com) for $2.1 billion. By then, my share was diluted down through the natural evolution of a startup—the A round, B round, and C round of investments—so my stake was no longer half. But as I look back, I realize that $1 billion of value came from that one meeting.

The lessons I took forward from that day are: first realize that not all meetings are scheduled. Sometimes, meetings come up spontaneously, especially when you are working in person with lots of people bumping into each other throughout the day.

Recognize that spontaneity is your friend. Often, we get caught up in our schedule, and we're determined to prepare for that next meeting, so we're not open to something that might come up. Your first reflex is to say no, or perhaps another time. Resist that and think, why not? Then if it feels right in your gut, say yes.

Second, this spontaneous meeting, by definition, has no agenda. I do believe that no meeting should be scheduled without an agenda. But exceptions must be made for special circumstances. I certainly didn't go into that impromptu lunch with Steve with any agenda. I didn't know that he'd make an offer to me. Steve didn't know this either. After all, he literally just met me.

Granted, we were introduced by a partner at a major venture firm who knew both of us. That's one sign that you should take this unexpected meeting and treat it seriously. Being introduced by a trusted friend or intermediary of any kind of can be shorthand for magic about to happen. While it's rare for an opportunity like this to be put on the table, that's the point. You never know where a new idea might lead, so going with your gut instinct will continue being vital in impromptu meetings.

Finally, having no preset agenda can be a great driver of a successful meeting. It's counterintuitive, because one of the first things we are typically taught is that the agenda is the most important item to have going into a meeting. Not always. Notice the give and take between me and Steve in that first meeting. We were exploring big ideas, with no agenda, and there was no way to plan a conversation like that ahead of time.

My takeaway from one of the most fateful days of my career was *not* to be on the lookout for impromptu meetings and try to make them happen by bumping into colleagues at random and asking them if they'd like to have a quick meeting now. That is not a good idea. Rather, the takeaway is this: be open to chance encounters, and follow your gut instinct from there.

Being Maniacal About Hiring and Meetings

At first, Kayak was incubated inside the offices of General Catalyst. Many one-on-one meetings with Steve established our working relationship to come. He would run the business side and I would run product development. We each put $1 million of our own money into the venture, and the venture capital firm made an initial seed investment of $5 million.

This first phase of the startup was exciting. Our meetings were shockingly fast, usually lasting just 5 or 10 minutes. And we were very aggressive in meetings about making decisions to the point where it sometimes seemed reckless. We both felt it was better to decide something than to debate it. So we were always trying stuff rapidly.

My bipolar condition came into play. I was first diagnosed with bipolar illness at age 25. Some of my symptoms seemed advantageous at the time. I could be highly productive, go days at a time with tiny amounts of sleep, and I wrote prolifically.

I didn't talk about it publicly back then, but over the past decade I have spoken openly about it—to try and help others and understand how it has affected my life and career. For as long as I can remember, I've experienced highs and lows in my mood, but friends told me that I wasn't bipolar given the diagnostic definitions. My highs were less elevated. My "up" moods rarely reached full-blown "mania."

This made sense when I was diagnosed with bipolar II disorder, in which the less-intense "hypomanic" episodes are often quite pleasant to be around. According to the Mayo Clinic, those with bipolar II can often seem like the life of the party—making jokes, taking an intense interest in other people and activities, and infecting others with their positive mood. For my hypomanic spells, I could "feel the fire" spreading through my body, giving me that feeling of being driven to reach my visions.

However, there was a negative side that started catching up with me: I had grandiosity, I was easily irritated by people whom I perceived as not being "fast" enough, I drank too much, and I was very impulsive. During depressive episodes, I spent days on the floor, and had panic attacks, and was fearful that night would not turn into day, and that my bad days were going to be here forever.

Sometimes being bipolar has been good to me; it has led me to new friends and relationships. And I've gotten feedback that my story has helped others. However, sometimes this has been bad for me. I've heard through backchannels that some business partners worry about what it would be like to go into business with someone who is bipolar.

It's why I believed it was important to put boundaries around my work life. I didn't want to be the kind of person who has a manic vision in the middle of the night or on a Sunday morning and starts texting or emailing my colleagues. Steve and I believed in the work-hard, play-hard concept where we worked with intensity from Monday to Friday, 9 a.m. to 5 p.m. In our decade at Kayak, I hardly ever spoke to Steve nights and weekends—maybe once per year—except on business trips, when we would hang out for dinner and drinks.

One example of making a rash, seemingly reckless decision had to do with choosing the name of the company. When we were several months old, we hired a brand agency in New York to come up with our name. From their list of options presented in a meeting, we picked out Kayak. I like just the look of the word. I liked that it's five letters and that it's a palindrome spelled the same forward and backward. I had read somewhere—maybe in a book by advertising legend David Ogilvy—that the letter *K* is very valuable in branding. Witness the successful launch of classic brands such as Kleenex, Kraft, Kodak, Keds, and Special K from Kellogg's.

Steve and I went back to our board and said we had chosen to name the company. One of the partners at General Catalyst said, "You'll name the company Kayak over my dead body. That's a completely stupid name. He thought people would be distracted and think we're only adventure travel." We said thank you, and I immediately ignored the objection. We acquired the domain name kayak.com for $30,000 and moved ahead with our new identity.

Steve moved his newly formed business team into offices in Norwalk, Connecticut, a great place to be for going into Manhattan for business development and partner meetings without having to pay New York City rents. I moved my budding engineering team into offices in an office park in Concord, Massachusetts, located a few miles from the Old North Bridge, the site of the "shot heard round the world" that triggered the Revolutionary War. Steve came to Concord once a week, and I went to either Connecticut or New York, where he was, once every couple of weeks.

In both locations, we were maniacally focused on two things: meetings and hiring. I had both floors of our Concord location designed as open spaces, where there were no private offices and the conference rooms had glass walls, as well as a kitchen with free drinks, snacks, and high-end coffee machines, and beers on Friday afternoons. It meant we'd be spending a lot of time in each other's presence.

From the start, I was hyper-focused on personally recruiting and interviewing and assigning tests and tasks to candidates to find the best A-level talent. I wanted only programmers who knew how to write high-quality code quickly and who were also good people to be around. For me, businesses exist as an excuse to get a team together, and product is what a team does. Six of the first 12 people I hired stayed with me not only at Kayak but at my next startups over the next decade.

My right-hand person, Paul Schwenk, was already a loyal colleague from earlier in my career. He helped me arrange the desks in arrays according to job tasks and also kept the loudest people apart from each other so the office didn't get too noisy. Schwenk and I became obsessed with designing a user interface (UI) for Kayak that was simpler and faster than any other travel site. We wanted a UI so simple that super busy could use it, with software so fast that someone trying to do many things at once won't have time to be distracted away from it.

We took these demands to chief engineer Bill O'Donnell, who at first said what we wanted was impossible. But he and the team ended up doing it, making Kayak known for setting a new standard for speed and simplicity in travel searching. "Billo," as everyone came to call him, also became a lifelong friend and colleague.

When it came to meetings, I stood outside conference rooms with a tally clicker used for product inventory. I believed strongly in small meetings that were as short as possible. There would be no 10-person meetings at Kayak. If I clicked on more than three people going into a meeting, I would intervene to identify the nonessential people and toss them out of the room to go back to work at their desks.

My question was always: What is the right group of three? From my days at Intuit, I knew that three was the optimal number for effective meetings in which action points were debated and decisions were made. Only on special occasions would we have larger, company-wide meetings to share news on hitting milestones.

This combination of being maniacal about hiring and meetings paid off in terms of our speed and productivity. Only about four months went by between the launch of our startup in January 2004 to our very first beta test product, which was flight search only. The website was ready for testing by May 5, 2004. We held a party meeting to celebrate Cinco de Mayo with a round of Mexican beers, chips, and salsa. Then, after five months of getting feedback from test users and debugging the software, we were ready for our initial flights-only product launch by October. Our biggest advantage was the Google-like simplicity of our user interface, especially if you contrasted it with the overwhelming complexity of all the graphics and promotions displayed on the home pages of all the other major travel sites.

By then our practice of impromptu meetings underwent a transition to a more formalized meeting culture. Every conference room had a tally clicker hanging on the doorknob to remind everyone about the small meetings rule. The main conference room had a stuffed elephant, named Annabell, sitting on a shelf, to represent "the elephant in the room," the big issue that couldn't be avoided and had to be confronted and solved in the meeting.

Solving the Business Model Challenge

As we ramped up from a handful of developers to a peak of 200 employees, meetings took on greater and greater importance. To run daily operations, I relied heavily on Schwenk, who did everything from coordinating with the Connecticut office to manage all finances and purchasing to keeping programmers from wasting time playing video games to fixing the plumbing. Schwenk often describes himself as my opposite. "Paul is the innovation guy, the inspiration," Schwenk often says. "He comes up with a million ideas constantly. I'm more of the 'let's get the trains running and keep them running' kind of guy."

Often, Schwenk was in the position of saying no to my whims or to employee requests that otherwise seemed fine by me. No, he'd say, we're not sending the entire company on an off-site trip to the Bahamas. No, we're not spending $8,000 on an exotic lamp that Paul thinks is cool. The Connecticut office granted employees the day off on summer Fridays. "I said no," Schwenk recalls. "We're not doing that here in Concord. If you want a day off, take it as a day off." Schwenk was even disciplined at lunch time and was known for brown paper bagging it at his desk.

As a result of Schwenk's controls, the company wasn't wasting our investor money. Yet we struggled out of the gate to reach profitability.

The biggest challenge was the underlying business model, which a year into the venture didn't appear to be working. It was costing $1 to attract the average visitor to Kayak.com, yet the company was earning only 20 cents on referral fees for that customer. This was primarily due to the low commissions on flight sales that airlines paid out. But it was also due to the cost of development and marketing and the methods that Kayak was using to gather real-time flight booking data and pricing. Lacking a direct link to a real-time data feed, Kayak had to "scrape" the flight times and prices from all the airline websites and constantly import it into Kayak.com. This caused Kayak to swamp those airline sites with waves of traffic to the point where it crashed Delta.com, angering a major carrier.

In meetings, we needed to focus on solving the business model challenge. Yet I was often preoccupied with other things. This is how Schwenk tells it if he's asked when I'm not around: "Paul has a very short attention span, if you haven't figured that out already," Schwenk would say to our colleagues. "And so you can't go into meetings and just babble back and forth, because Paul gets bored. He needs to be engaged, and you have to be on point, and you have to get stuff decided and planned out in these meetings."

In those early days of Kayak, when most meetings were impromptu and the agendas were on-the-fly, Schwenk's disciplined approach to meetings with me and Steve Hafner made up for my shortcomings. That discipline drove the way meetings were handled and how tasks were prioritized. Schwenk would always ask, "All right, we have a million things to do. We can't do it all at once. What do we have to do? And what's the top priority?"

To fix the business model issue, the priorities were set: First, move as quickly as possible into hotel search. With standard commissions of 10–20% on each search that led to a direct booking with a Hilton or a Hyatt or a booking on any other travel site, it meant Kayak would collect an average of $80 on a $200 room for a two-night stay. Compare that to commissions of only $1 or $2 for an airline booking. Rental car bookings were also quite profitable, but those would only end up accounting for about 8% of search traffic over the years. The big money was in hotels.

Second, Kayak had to figure out a way to establish real-time data links with all the major travel suppliers, to avoid the costly process of scrapping the data and thus antagonizing our biggest partners. But that problem was more strategic and required a longer-term plan, whereas the move into hotel search required speed and agility.

For every meeting we had about launching our hotel product, we'd spend 15–20 minutes digging into a problem or issue, make a decision on what to do, and then get it done. On this, everyone at the company agreed: you make the decision, then you go with it. The decision may be wrong, but it can be fixed later. As long as it's fast. We had incredible engineers, and we could go really fast. We'd prototype something and throw it out to the customers. If it failed to work, we changed it quickly. Meetings drove that efficiency. Most meetings were short and went superfast. By the middle of 2005, Kayak launched our global hotel search product. Traffic exploded, and big commissions started flowing.

For the second, more strategic problem, Kayak's leadership team decided they needed to court the founders of another local travel startup called ITA Software. Based in Cambridge, ITA was founded in 2001 by Jeremy Wertheimer, a computer scientist from MIT's Artificial Intelligence Labs who hired the most brilliant programmers he could find. They figured out how to program those real-time feeds with all the travel companies, a system that became known as QPX. Meeting with Jerry and ITA's leadership team required skillful negotiation. We needed to integrate QPX into Kayak under a continual use agreement, but Kayak needed to get it without overpaying.

Once this happened, and with hotel bookings flowing, Kayak was performing more than a million searches per day, and the company was growing bigger and bigger. Since Kayak didn't have to service the booking, a major customer service cost center wasn't necessary. If the customer had to change their flight or hotel itinerary or experienced a flight delay, they'd call the airline or hotel or Expedia or whoever made the booking. Still, Kayak customers would sometimes encounter glitches or experience problems with Kayak itself, such as price discrepancies with other websites, and so there needed to be a customer support function. The leadership team decided against hiring dedicated customer support people and instead it was either me or any of the engineers who would answer the red phone that we designated for our support line.

Many of the problems that customers reported required meetings to fix the issue. I actually loved taking calls from irate customers, because it put a challenge in my head. I was always thinking, *How do I convert them to a customer who loves us?*

But this kind of customer support doesn't scale. Eventually, I worked with team members to build an entire email infrastructure system for support that would assign each problem to a team member. I would get a couple of problems per day, Schwenk and Billo would get a couple, and then engineers would get the rest. We had to find out what the problem was and respond to the customer as soon as possible.

The Challenge of Growing Bigger

By 2007, we had grown into a mid-sized company, and we started having bigger meetings. You have to schedule them because there's more people involved. Sometimes lawyers or finance people from Connecticut were involved. We'd now require that every meeting have an agenda in advance. Yet it was beginning to feel that we could no longer accomplish anything quickly, because there were too many stakeholders.

I was always beating the drum of speed, that we had to make decisions quickly, that we needed to have quick turnarounds when addressing problems and opportunities. The biggest opportunity came with the introduction of the iPhone and Apple's App Store. We did a full-court press to develop a smartphone app version of Kayak. Launched in 2008 without any new marketing for the app, it was downloaded by 35 million customers over the next four years.

In 2010, Google offered to acquire our key partner ITA Software for $700 million. When I heard that number, I set a new target for what Kayak was worth. After all, ITA supplied the inner database links that the end-user customer never really saw. We were providing the user interface and the brand, which I believed was worth much more. I set a target of being worth double ITA, that we wouldn't sell Kayak for less than $1.4 billion.

The proposed Google acquisition also set off an immediate challenge. What if Google cut us off from ITA's QPX system? Without the real-time links to the travel suppliers, we'd have to go back to scraping their websites, which couldn't easily happen at our current scale. We objected to the acquisition with the US Department of Justice, which put us in meetings with high-level government officials for the first time. Our petition led to an agreement that

Google had to license access to QPX to outside parties at a reasonable rate for at least the next five years. With that, the acquisition went through, and Google was now our new partner, which gave us more credibility heading into our initial public stock offering (IPO).

We used our meeting culture to drive speed and efficiency all the way up until we went public in July 2012, when we raised $91 million from our IPO on the Nasdaq. That put our valuation in the hundreds of millions. Our fast turnaround times had paid off for our investors. And we managed to hold on to our people. We had the same core people, the same engineers, the same quality assurance staff, the same operations people all through those years. They'd instill the meeting culture onto the new people who were joining Kayak. As a result, we didn't have long release cycles, we were releasing improved versions of the website and the app on a constant basis.

Yet under chief software architect Billo, we also managed to do all this within normal work hours. No one was working 60, 70, or 80 hours per week, like you'd hear at other software startups. That prevented burnout and enabled us to keep our people loyal, staying with us for years, which also lowered recruiting costs.

As such, our meeting culture was intertwined with our operational efficiency. When we compared ourselves to travel competitors, we were off the charts. For a time, Steve Hafner wanted us to acquire Orbitz, where he had previously worked. We found out that Orbitz had 900 people in software engineering at the same time we had fewer than 50. A lot of companies bloat up like that. The minute they make money or raise a lot of money, they go on a hiring spree. By contrast, Kayak had no bloat. We kept teams and meetings small, with clear agendas and tasks to get done. We decided that there's no way we could acquire Orbitz because our cultures would be too incompatible.

In the end, when Priceline, later renamed Booking.com, acquired Kayak for about $2 billion in 2014, we had 200 employees, which meant our market value per employee averaged $10 million each, which is insane. But the figure I like to use is $1.5 million revenue per employee, as we were generating $300 million in revenue with that staff of 200. Still, that figure is off-the-charts efficient for a company of any size. I attribute that success to our original passion for being maniacal about hiring and meetings.

CHAPTER 5

How Airbnb Created a New Kind of Company

Ilove the saying "a stranger is just a friend I haven't yet met," often attributed to Irish poet William Butler Yeats but also to Will Rogers and to many hosts of Airbnb's around the world. It's especially amazing to me that this became the founding idea of a new kind of company. It all started in fall 2007, when a pair of 26-year-old buddies, Brian Chesky and Joe Gebbia, found themselves struggling to pay the rent for their small San Francisco apartment. The city's hotels were fully booked due to an upcoming design conference, and the friends saw an unusual opportunity.

The housemates decided to turn their living room into a lodging space for conference attendees who couldn't find a hotel room. They bought three air mattresses, set them up on the hardwood floor and called their idea AirBed & Breakfast. The first guests, a 30-something woman, a father from Utah, and an Indian student, paid $80 each to sleep on the airbeds and get breakfast in the morning. More than the money, what struck Brian and Joe was the human connection: strangers becoming friends over a simple home-cooked meal and a place to stay. They felt they'd stumbled onto something bigger than a quick fix for rent.

The two teamed up with a former roommate, Nathan Blecharczyk, a coder with a knack for building things fast. In 2008, the three founders officially launched a website that let people rent out airbeds or spare rooms in their homes. But the timing seemed terrible: the US economy was crashing, people were losing their homes, and trust in strangers was not exactly at an all-time high. From a meeting with the three founders came the idea that they needed a big test of their concept. The Democratic National Convention in Denver that same year fit the bill. Hotels were sold out again, and the trio convinced locals to list their spaces on the site. They got a few hundred bookings, but when the convention ended, bookings vanished. Investors weren't interested. One famously told them, "I hope that's not the only idea you're working on."

The three founders huddled once again. Strapped for cash, they came up with a quirky idea: sell novelty cereal boxes. They designed special "Obama O's" and "Cap'n McCain" boxes during the 2008 election and sold them for $40 each. The stunt brought in about $30,000, enough to keep Airbnb alive for a few more months, and it caught the eye of Paul Graham at the startup accelerator Y Combinator. Graham didn't believe in the business at first but was impressed by their hustle. He told them if they could get people to buy cereal, they could probably get people to stay in each other's homes.

In early 2009, Airbnb joined Y Combinator. The founders spent those months visiting hosts in New York City, one of their few active markets, and realized many listings had terrible photos. They rented a camera and went door-to-door, shooting high-quality pictures of people's apartments. Bookings doubled almost immediately.

They learned a core lesson: good design and trust-building details could turn skepticism into bookings. Slowly, Airbnb's listings grew from couches and airbeds to entire apartments, houses, and unique stays: treehouses, yurts, boats. By 2011, they had over a million nights booked. By 2012, they were expanding globally, opening offices in London, Paris, Moscow, São Paulo, and beyond.

Yet with growth came backlash. Cities around the world grappled with the question: Was Airbnb helping people make ends meet, or fueling illegal hotels and housing shortages? Neighbors complained about parties and noise. Hotel groups lobbied for tighter regulations, arguing Airbnb hosts didn't follow the same safety or tax rules. In places like New York, Barcelona, and Berlin, heated legal battles played out.

That set off a series of meetings that resulted in a response that guides the company to this day. They would aim to position the company as a community, not just a booking platform. They rolled out a "Host Guarantee" to protect hosts against damages, introduced guest reviews, and invested in a sleek, friendly design language that emphasized belonging. The 2014 rebrand introduced the now-famous "Bélo" logo, symbolizing people, places, love, and trust. Their mission statement became "Belong Anywhere."

By the mid-2010s, Airbnb was valued in the tens of billions, a true Silicon Valley unicorn. It was more than a way to find cheap stays; it became a cultural phenomenon. Travelers wanted "authentic" local experiences instead of cookie-cutter hotel rooms. For hosts, Airbnb was a way to supplement income, meet people from around the world, and share a piece of their life.

Facing a Defining Crisis

When 2020 began, Airbnb was at a new peak. The company was preparing for an eagerly anticipated initial public offering (IPO) that would mark the culmination of over a decade of breakneck growth and global expansion. Chesky and his leadership team were thinking big: new product lines, business travel, luxury stays, and curated experiences were all part of Airbnb's expanding vision.

Then came COVID-19. Practically overnight, the idea of staying in strangers' homes, Airbnb's entire business model, became unthinkable for millions of people. Borders closed. Flights were grounded. Hosts saw their bookings evaporate. Guests demanded refunds. The company, which once seemed unstoppable, lost 80% of its revenue in a matter of weeks.

Inside Airbnb, what happened next was an intense test of leadership under crisis. Chesky would later call it "the most harrowing experience of my life." In March 2020, as the reality of the pandemic set in, the top executives gathered, now virtually, for emergency meetings that would stretch late into the night. There were no playbooks for what they faced. Chesky, Blecharczyk, and Gebbia met multiple times every day with chief financial officer Dave Stephenson trying to stabilize a company suddenly on the brink.

They confronted stark questions: How do you handle millions of canceled reservations? How do you support hosts whose livelihoods are disappearing? How do you cut costs so dramatically that you can survive, without destroying the culture that made the company special?

One of Chesky's early decisions was to refund guests whose trips were canceled due to the pandemic. It was a costly move. The company refunded nearly $1 billion, but they believed that putting trust and the community first was the only way to protect Airbnb's brand in the long run. This created another crisis: thousands of angry hosts, who suddenly lost income and felt abandoned. Chesky and the leadership team quickly scheduled virtual town halls and listening sessions with hosts worldwide. One executive described those meetings as "painful but clarifying," because they forced Airbnb to reckon with the true meaning of "belonging" when money was tight.

Internally, the daily executive meetings were raw. Chesky described them as a crash course in ruthless prioritization. They used a whiteboard approach: if it wasn't absolutely essential, it was paused or cut. The leadership team reviewed every line of spending and every team function.

By May 2020, it became clear that layoffs were inevitable. Chesky gathered his top executives for a final call on how deep the cuts would go. They decided on a painful but deliberate approach: about 25% of employees, about

1,900 people, would lose their jobs. But they resolved to handle it differently than typical Silicon Valley cuts. In a series of internal meetings, they planned every detail: generous severance, health insurance extensions, laptops left with departing employees, and support for finding new jobs, all to preserve trust and dignity.

Chesky's layoff letter to employees became widely shared as a model of transparency and empathy. It was the result of multiple late-night revisions with his closest team, who believed that honesty was the only way forward. In the same period, Airbnb paused all its splashy projects, like its flights and transportation ambitions, and focused instead on its core: helping everyday people share their homes.

Another focus of the leadership's daily meetings was reimagining what Airbnb could be in a world where people were scared to travel. The executive team used regular brainstorming sessions, often just Chesky and a few product leaders on marathon Zoom calls, to ask, what do people want now? The answer turned out to be simple but powerful: longer stays, closer to nature, and flexibility.

Instead of urban short-term stays for tourists, they pivoted to "living anywhere," entire homes for weeks or months. They rolled out new search filters for remote work stays and upgraded their cleaning protocols to reassure guests. They also cut or delayed flashy new bets and instead doubled down on core technology, trust, and safety.

Throughout 2020, the top leadership continued to meet every day, even weekends. Chesky said later that the constant cadence kept them aligned when the news was changing by the hour. They abandoned PowerPoints and formality, meetings were frank, often emotional, sometimes exhausting. One executive later described it as "a startup inside a giant company again."

Their bet started to pay off. People were not traveling for business or city weekends, but families were renting cabins, countryside homes, and beach houses for extended stays. Rural bookings surged. Airbnb's business, while battered, stabilized faster than traditional hotels.

In the weeks leading up to December 2020, the leadership team reconvened for one of their biggest decisions yet: whether to go ahead with the IPO. They debated the risk, COVID was still raging, vaccines were only beginning to roll out, and markets were unpredictable. But after weeks of tense calls with bankers and investors, Chesky and his senior team agreed: going public was the right move. The IPO would raise cash, reward loyal employees and investors, and prove Airbnb was here to stay.

The offering was a triumph. On its first day of trading, Airbnb's stock price more than doubled, briefly valuing the company at over $100 billion. Many on the leadership team reflected that this milestone would not have happened if they hadn't stripped the company back to its roots during those brutal months.

Airbnb emerged from COVID's worst period as a leaner, more focused company. Its leadership's relentless internal meetings during the crisis redefined what mattered most: trust, hosts, guests, and a sense of belonging. Gone were the flashy expansions into unrelated businesses. What survived was the original idea that started on three air mattresses in San Francisco: that a home, and the people who share it, could make travel feel human again, even in the hardest of times. A company that nearly collapsed under a pandemic's weight became a different kind of company, one that learned, painfully, how to focus on what really matters.

Why Meeting Agendas and Moderators Are Essential

By 2022, after COVID let up, millions of knowledge workers had an opportunity to reimagine what the word *workplace* meant. While some clung to the hope that cubicles and open-plan offices would again buzz with daily foot traffic, Airbnb embraced a new promise: homes could be permanent offices, too. And yet, as cofounder Nate Blecharczyk told me, unlocking a flexible work model is only half the story. The other half is ensuring that the backbone of any company, its meeting culture, doesn't fall apart in the process. After all, bad meetings are costly. And if there's one thing Airbnb's story shows, it's that meeting culture, like travel itself, must be intentionally designed.

It begins with the most popular kind of meeting: the regularly scheduled team huddle. "Recurring meetings run the risk of just going on autopilot," Nate says. When a standing one-on-one or team check-in appears on the calendar each week, it often becomes ritual rather than progress. The agenda becomes the guardrail that keeps the conversation productive.

At Airbnb, leaders must draft and send out agendas for every meeting in advance. The reasons are practical: without a clear plan, people waste precious time trying to remember updates on the spot. With an agenda, both sides know what matters, what decisions or feedback are needed, and where the conversation should steer. This discipline scales up. For larger group meetings, the same principle applies: come prepared or risk drifting. In fast-moving companies where calendars are crowded and information is fluid, this small habit can spell the difference between a meeting that clarifies and one that confuses.

But structure is not only about bullet points. Airbnb leaders know a good meeting demands someone to protect that structure. That's where moderation comes in. "A good meeting needs a moderator," Nate explains, "someone who really takes charge to steer the conversation." He knows firsthand how easy it is for a seemingly focused discussion to spiral. A tangent here, a "quick thought" there, and suddenly the core agenda is buried under a mountain of side trails.

The moderator's role is partly practical, a timekeeper, a traffic cop for ideas. But it's also diplomatic. A well-trained moderator must gently intercept rabbit holes without shutting down valuable insight. A moderator should also solicit input from the most relevant people, especially if those voices are getting spoken over or effectively cut out of the conversation.

This balancing act can be tough, especially when the participants don't all sit in the same hierarchy. "Depending on who's leading the meeting," says Nate, "there could be politics about whether that person really feels empowered to control the conversation." In his case, being a cofounder comes with a built-in authority to guide a cross-functional room. Others must develop the soft power to do the same, creating psychological safety while keeping the meeting on the rails.

The Small-Group Imperative

Equally important is who's invited in the first place. Airbnb's rule of thumb is one that I also champion: keep meetings as small as possible, but not so small that key voices are left out. It's an age-old dilemma for managers. Leave people out, and you risk silos, when decisions get made in the dark, forcing redundant follow-ups to fill in those who missed out. But include everyone, and the room fills with bystanders who sit in silence and burn time.

Nate offers a simple test: "If it's a situation where you're going to have a meeting, but people who are in attendance don't participate, then they probably didn't need to be there. They could have gotten the notes afterwards."

Why the Hybrid Is the Hardest

If moderating a big room is tricky, moderating a hybrid one is even trickier. "Meetings work well if everyone's in the room or if everyone's on Zoom," Nate says. "Hybrid is challenging." There are audio lags, poor mics, people talking over one another for half a second. Remote participants strain to see who's speaking. Nuance, tone, and side comments get lost. And the subtle cues of in-person dynamics, eye contact, reading the room are invisible behind a pixelated screen.

"This has remained an unsolved challenge," says Nate. "Microphones can be improved and fancy cameras can isolate individual participants simultaneously, but communication doesn't always feel smooth. The problem is worse the bigger the room and the number of participants."

Improvements are always needed since the fully in-person meeting has nearly vanished at Airbnb. "One hundred percent of meetings are either fully remote or hybrid," Nate says.

The On-Site Is the New Off-Site

Underpinning all this is Airbnb's new philosophy about where work happens. For the company that revolutionized where people sleep, it's fitting that it now experiments with where people work. "The off-site is the new on-site," Nate says. In the Airbnb universe, the standard workweek is remote by default. Before the pandemic: off-sites were held in (Airbnb) homes, and day-to-day work in the office. After the pandemic: day-to-day work happens at the employee's home, and off-sites happen in the office. Yet the goals remain the same: build trust, relationships, and creative energy.

How Road Maps Drive Narrative Arcs

If meetings are the heartbeat of daily operations, road maps are the company's long-term compass. Airbnb's version is distinctive for its mix of structure and fluidity. Twice a year, about 75–100 key people gather to review the road map. These sessions aren't designed to be final judgment days for product bets. They're more like forums to "socialize plans and identify concerns." If an idea sparks a wave of questions, it's not decided on the spot. Instead, follow-ups drill deeper, ensuring the right people tackle the right risks.

The road map itself unfolds in narrative arcs. Instead of launching isolated features, Airbnb bundles them on themes that speak to the cultural moment: "affordability during inflation," became a major narrative arc in the post-COVID world. This thematic coherence keeps product and marketing in lockstep, telling a story to both customers and employees.

For the next 6–18 months, the road map is detailed and specific. Beyond that, it's more directional, leaving room for market shifts or strategic pivots. This balance prevents teams from drifting into tunnel vision or building brittle plans that can't adapt.

The Twin Engines: Product and Marketing

In our series of conversations, Nate emphasized to me that Airbnb's product and marketing teams are joined at the hip from idea to launch. It's not a pipeline where engineers build and marketers scramble to spin up a story at the end. Instead, both functions look outward together, mapping what's happening in culture to what the company can deliver.

This integrated mindset surfaces again in launch moments. Every six months, Airbnb doesn't just ship features; it drops a cohesive narrative into the market. Customers don't see a jumble of updates; they see Airbnb responding to their needs in a clear, resonant theme.

"Correspondingly," says Nate, "we do a road map review every six months and that's where we bring together 75–100 people who are most consequential in terms of delivering the road map over the next 6, 12, or 18 months." This way, everybody sticks to six-month increments. Those responsible for delivering the road map aren't necessarily the most senior people in the company. It's not exclusively a hierarchy in the sense of who's doing the work.

The road map milestone meetings happen in person every six months in San Francisco. "This is the opportunity to really socialize what we're going to commit ourselves to. And if anyone has a problem with that, you want to know it now so that it can be dealt with and addressed."

A Blueprint for Modern Collaboration

Taken together, these practices reveal a blueprint for how to collaborate in the post-COVID, Zoom-infused world in which we find ourselves. Whether you run a startup or a global brand, the questions Airbnb asks are universal:

- ◆ Does this meeting have a purpose and an agenda that proves it?
- ◆ Are the right people here? Are the wrong people here?
- ◆ Is there a moderator empowered to keep us on track?

- Are decisions being made? Is information being cascaded to others afterwards?
- Is our hybrid setup helping or hindering real participation?
- How do we use in-person time intentionally instead of by default?
- Does our road map guide our work, or does it box us in?

The answers may look different for each company, but the core insight is the same: meetings don't just happen. They are built, like any good product, with care, iteration, and constant feedback.

As Airbnb's evolution shows, the companies that thrive in a flexible, distributed world won't be the ones that pine for the old office. Nor will they be the ones that treat remote work as an excuse for chaos. Instead, they'll be the ones that do the hard, unglamorous work of redesigning the small moments, the daily stand-ups, the cross-team brainstorms, the biannual road map summits. They'll make off-sites matter more than on-sites ever did. They'll trust people to work from anywhere, but never leave them to drift alone. And if they do it well, they'll find that the same spirit that unlocked millions of homes for travel can unlock millions of homes for work, and millions of hours saved from the meetings that don't deserve to happen.

To me, a key takeaway from Airbnb's story is that the future of work isn't remote versus the office. It's about how we gather, whether online or off, and how we make every gathering count. Airbnb's experience shows that getting this right isn't rocket science, it's design and discipline. Clear agendas. Small groups. Strong moderators. Hybrid setups that actually work. And above all, a mindset that *collaboration isn't a given, it's a design problem.*

Making All Meetings Count

If there's one overriding challenge from Airbnb's approach, it's this: every meeting should justify its existence. Every gathering, whether on a screen or around a firepit at an off-site, should earn the time it takes. When that happens, work stops being something that happens in spite of bad meetings. It happens because of great ones.

Brian believes that great meetings are central to belonging, creativity, and operational clarity. Along those lines, the leadership team at Airbnb has adopted a set of sometimes surprising best practices for its meeting culture. For Brian, it includes the rejection of one-on-one meetings.

Over time, the founding CEO came to dread one-on-one meetings with direct reports, calling them "flawed" and likening them to therapy sessions, where the employee "owns the agenda" and the boss becomes a listener rather than a strategist. He sees these as inefficient for sharing key information that others should also hear, so he prefers group forums where broader alignment happens.

Calendar overload is a barrier to that alignment. Back in the mid-2010s, Airbnb experimented with a "calendar amnesty," wiping everyone's meetings to reduce clutter, but this was short-lived. What emerged instead was a strong meeting hygiene culture (clear purpose, strict agendas), leaner, more effective working teams, often 10-people or fewer. When meetings happen, they are high-impact, decision-focused, not status-driven or info-heavy.

During COVID, when everything at Airbnb needed to be rebooted, Chesky entered back into "founder mode," a hands-on, detail-obsessed style influenced by Steve Jobs and Walt Disney. He pivoted from delegation to monitoring 75–80 projects weekly, not via one-on-ones, but through group project reviews. In all meetings, he encouraged open group discussions, mentorship, and visibility. The policy is that anyone can challenge decisions in public forums. That served to counterbalance the power that Chesky was exercising by going back into founder mode.

Post-pandemic, as Airbnb embraced remote and hybrid environments, Chesky banned early-morning meetings before 10 a.m. to respect rhythms and efficiency. Their tools included quarterly in-person gatherings ("immersive weeks") to foster connection in hybrid contexts. A norm of avoiding emails, pushing toward real-time engagement in meetings or in Slack chat channels.

Meetings are for action, not status updates. Airbnb targets meetings when high-stakes decisions or collective clarity are needed. Chesky favors visible, group-level feedback, dragging conversations into the open.

Scheduling should be thoughtful. Quarterly physical meetups help create empathy due to personal interactions. For hybrid and remote meetings across time zones, choose a time for the meeting that isn't too early or too late in the day, as a way to signal empathy even before the meeting starts.

Using these tools, Airbnb's meeting culture has transformed from endless one-on-ones and calendar bloat to embracing an agenda-centric approach with a trust-driven group, with founder mode getting activated during a crisis.

Designing Meetings and Travel Experiences

Another role of the founder is to come up with the next big thing. In late 2016, Brian embarked on what he saw as a bold bet, wagering that it wasn't enough to help travelers find a place to stay. What if Airbnb could help them discover what to *do* once they arrived?

That question gave birth to Airbnb Experiences, a product designed to unlock cities through the eyes of local artists, chefs, surfers, historians, the people with the kind of knowledge you couldn't get from a guidebook. The idea was simple but radical: turn the host into a local insider if they weren't one already.

Nearly a decade later, Experiences has become Airbnb's highest-rated offering, with over 90% of reviews landing at five stars, outpacing even its iconic home listings. But the journey hasn't been a straight line. From the pandemic pause to a major relaunch, the story of Experiences reveals how Airbnb designs products: with vision, discipline, and an unwavering belief that the best ideas start by working backward from the customer.

Every big idea at Airbnb starts the same way: with a memo. Not a PowerPoint deck. Not a spreadsheet full of quarterly targets. But a tightly argued, two- to four-page narrative that lays out what could be, as inspired by Amazon's legendary "six-pager" approach. Brian writes these memos like a story. They're aspirational, demanding, and designed to push teams beyond incremental tweaks. It's Airbnb's way of forcing everyone to think bigger: What does this product look like in 10 years, not 10 months?

The company's planning horizon stretches far beyond the next launch cycle. Big products can take two years from memo to reality, with 18 months of development and up to three years mapped out on the master road map. That road map ticks forward like clockwork: a major launch every six months, whether it's a new feature for homes or a new version of Experiences.

Inside Airbnb, there's a simple rule: start with the experience you want the customer to have, then work backward until it's possible. For Experiences, this meant asking, *How do we give guests access to moments they could never find on TripAdvisor or Google Maps?* The answer wasn't to repurpose mass tours or big bus operators. It was to find real locals with unique stories to share, the cheesemaker in Tuscany, the DJ in Tokyo, the street artist in São Paulo.

That vision created a product unlike anything else in the travel market, one that had to be curated, moderated, and nurtured like a living marketplace. And it demanded that product teams, marketing, and local supply all work in sync from day one.

If Airbnb's Experiences product proves anything, it's that bold ideas need more than vision. They need disciplined execution. That discipline doesn't just live in road maps and memos. It lives in the everyday rhythms of how people gather, talk, and decide what to do next.

Inside Airbnb's top leadership circle, that rhythm is intentional. Every week, the executive team, known simply as the E Team, blocks out up to three hours to align on the road map and check that projects are tracking toward the bigger picture. It's not a ceremonial gathering. It's a working session that keeps strategy connected to reality.

But just because meetings happen regularly doesn't mean they should happen automatically. Airbnb tracks a surprising statistic: about 25% of one-on-one meetings get canceled when the agenda is thin. That's not a failure but rather a sign that time isn't wasted when there's nothing meaningful to discuss. A good meeting isn't about filling the calendar. It's about adding value.

For the urgent moments when waiting for a slot just won't cut it, Airbnb keeps it simple: just text. An immediate text policy for fast-moving or crisis issues keeps the company responsive without piling on unnecessary calls. When you run a global platform with real-world impact, from local trust and safety to natural disaster response, speed matters.

Inclusivity matters, too. That's why Airbnb's "hot topics" process lets team members add their own agenda items before the E-Team sits down. It's a simple tweak that opens the door to ideas and updates that might otherwise get buried. And it ensures the room stays connected to what's happening on the ground. These small cultural signals add up to an operating model built for agility. The best protection against chaos is clarity—especially when it comes to adapting to the unexpected, whether it's wildfires or new city regulations or sudden surges in demand or simply keeping a huge, distributed workforce aligned.

Past crises taught them that good intentions aren't enough. Structure, data, and trust in people's judgment are what keep the wheels turning when the world turns upside down. That's why the company continually refines how information flows, how decisions get made, and who's empowered to lead.

It all comes back to the core concepts that continue to guide Experiences: the road maps in six-month increments, the narrative memos, and that when it comes to meetings, good design beats default design. Great meetings don't happen because they're on the calendar. Great collaboration doesn't happen because everyone has Wi-Fi. They happen because leaders choose to make them happen with vision, with discipline, and with the humility to keep improving every week.

You can tell that I admire the meeting culture of Airbnb quite a bit. I can tell that it's true because it makes me a bit teary-eyed to think that their meeting culture was designed based on that big human-centric belief about how strangers can become friends. But it's also about driving innovation. If the future of travel is about belonging anywhere, as Airbnb says, the future of work at Airbnb is about making sure every meeting, every plan, every conversation earns its place, so that big, bold ideas don't just stay as ideas but become reality.

CHAPTER 6

How LinkedIn Was Built on Better Meetings

In December 2002, Reid Hoffman invited four other Silicon Valley tech execs to a meeting at his rented house in Mountain View. An avid role-play gamer as a kid who started his career in product design for Apple and later ran business development for PayPal, Hoffman aimed to flesh out an idea for a new website for professional networking. Sitting cross-legged on the carpet in the living room, the team that became the five cofounders of LinkedIn were convinced from the start that the working world needed a trusted network where relationships, not just résumés, opened doors to opportunities.

No one knew what that would look like, but there were plenty of ideas. As the founding CEO, Hoffman laid ground rules for meetings that would keep everyone focused on the goal of addressing the big question: How do we make professional networking digital and scalable, yet personal and trustworthy? This focus was essential given LinkedIn's initial market uncertainty. The founders didn't know its exact target audience. Was it for experienced professionals, recent graduates, frequent job-hoppers, for executive recruiters, or all of the above?

My relationship with Reid is based on a shared appreciation of how to set a vision for a startup that carries through as the company grows. To this day, he recalls talking to me in the early days of LinkedIn and notes that I was the first person outside of the company to recognize the founding vision: that LinkedIn wasn't just for an individual to make new connections but also to enable all the people in their network to do so. "Part of why I built it was that LinkedIn isn't just helping me," he says, "it's also helping the people in my network connect with each other." Over the years, Reid has always remained open to hearing my ideas for improving LinkedIn.

I've long admired the way Reid established a strong meeting culture at LinkedIn right from that first meeting, which went a long way toward setting the tone for everything that would come after. He championed rigorous, disciplined meetings by insisting that every person in the room, no matter their role, come prepared. He'd open meetings using a framework he got from his graduate school days at Oxford: What is the problem, what is the hypothesis, and what will we test first? "Good meetings aren't about consensus," Hoffman says, "they're about clarity."

The founding team mapped out the early product on butcher paper taped to the walls. They debated whether profiles should be public or only visible to members, whether connections should be one-way or mutual, and whether people would be comfortable putting their work history online at all. Hoffman knew that the product could only be built if the conversations were open, candid, and often uncomfortable.

From the start, he enforced three principles that became cornerstones of LinkedIn's meeting culture:

- Be intellectually honest. Present your idea backed up by data.
- Debate the idea, not the person. Egos kill good decisions.
- End with action. No meeting should conclude without clear next steps.

This translated into a culture where meetings had to have clear outcomes, whether that was a decision, an owner assigned to a task, or a strategy adjustment. To avoid letting meetings become a substitute for real work in those early LinkedIn days, he and the leadership team limited recurring meetings and focused on minimizing "meeting creep," where meetings multiply without clear purpose. Instead, Hoffman emphasized that meetings should accelerate decision-making and action. "Meetings are not for showing off intelligence. They are for aligning action." This way, meetings create momentum, rather than kill it.

Meetings as Trust Engines

As LinkedIn moved from idea to prototype, an expanding team of engineers, designers, and early salespeople crowded into Hoffman's house. They lacked office furniture, but they had whiteboards in every room and a stack of folding chairs that migrated from space to space. In those early months, Hoffman emphasized that meetings weren't about consensus, but clarity: "You want to get to a decision. It's fine if not everyone agrees, as long as they're heard." This informed LinkedIn's culture of "disagree and commit." Discussions could be contentious, but once a decision was made, everyone moved forward together.

In the very early days, for instance, one team member disagreed vehemently about including pictures in profiles. At the time, Facebook was about a year away from its initial launch for college students, and it would establish the profile picture as its central element. But there was no way to know this yet. There's a big reason not to have pictures, this team member argued. It's because we're not a dating site like Friendster. Profile pictures will make it all about attractiveness and will destroy our entire site. We'll go down in flames. It would be the end of LinkedIn.

After all arguments were heard, a decision was made that LinkedIn would indeed include profile pictures but that it would ban hitting on people. It had to be safe for working professionals. If a member reported that someone commented on their looks or asked them out on a date, it could be grounds for suspending the offending user. Thus, trust was reinforced by instituting a standard code of conduct that was distinct from other social networks.

Cofounder Allen Blue later recalled how Hoffman's approach to meetings forged trust in uncertain times. "When you're inventing something new," Blue said, "you don't have data yet. You have conversations. Those meetings were our data."

Only with the decisions forged in meetings would they be able to know what LinkedIn could become. After launching the first version in spring 2003, early beneficiaries were active networkers, recruiters, salespeople, and entrepreneurs who used it as a search tool. Hoffman emphasized LinkedIn's unique value proposition of aiding not just individual connections but also enabling existing networks of people to intertwine. Venture capital funded operations as the team busted out of Hoffman's house and moved into its first headquarters in Sunnyvale, California.

As LinkedIn grew, it became even more important that meetings were engines of mutual trust and transparency between employees and employers. LinkedIn meetings were expected to be open forums where employees could voice concerns or ask questions, especially of senior leadership. Company-wide stand-up meetings included live Q&A and votes by employees. Hoffman also believed in frequent, candid feedback, often exchanged in or after meetings. He viewed meetings as tools to reinforce cultural values like honesty. The reason was simple: if you can't build trust inside a room, you can't build trust outside it.

Large meetings at LinkedIn were like town halls. These stand-up meetings focused on operational status updates.

Only small, sit-down meetings became forums for debates where anyone could challenge an assumption. One engineer who had barely been onboarded once questioned whether the infamous "People You May Know" feature would feel invasive. Hoffman didn't shut him down. Instead, he made the engineer defend his concern and then assigned him to run an experiment to test how users felt.

This openness created a loop: meetings produced hypotheses, the team tested them fast, and results came back to the next meeting. This cadence of debating to testing to deciding made LinkedIn nimble in a market no one fully understood yet. As a result, it was a culture built for speed and agility rather than perfection. A strong proponent of the "launch fast and iterate" mindset, Hoffman became best known for his quote, "If you're not embarrassed by the first version of your product, you've launched too late."

This philosophy extended to meetings. Hoffman discouraged overpolished presentations or excessive preparation for internal meetings. Instead, teams were encouraged to use meetings to iterate and learn, not just showcase fully formed plans. One of the longest-running jokes about this set of early product meetings was centered on a feature for the Contact Finder search box. Back then, a decision was made to move ahead with launching it without a hotly debated "viral request" feature. Underscoring the value of moving ahead with speed, that feature remains nonlaunched more than two decades later, and nobody seems to miss it or remember what it was.

Crystalizing this as a general principle, meetings should not be roadblocks but instead tools for moving fast. Over the years, Hoffman has become more precise on when it's time to move. "Entrepreneurs should be prepared to make decisions with only 70% of the information they wish they had," he says. After that threshold, additional information won't significantly improve confidence. "Waiting for 90% might mean you're too late."

Determining the Business Model

It took reaching a network density of two million global users—a threshold crossed in February 2005—for LinkedIn to become generally useful for its intended purposes. As Hoffman puts it, "Once the network gets dense enough, which is roughly a couple million people globally, then, all of a sudden, it starts being useful for all kinds of things."

By then, the question of the business model became paramount. Now that millions of professionals have created profiles, how would LinkedIn make some real money? Only with data would they even know what users value most and what features could be developed as premiums that could justify charging fees. The question was urgent because the venture was running out of cash.

While it was already established that LinkedIn was free to join, and that it would make money through premium services, the company also established a rule that once something is offered free, it never becomes paid. "We could add paid features," Hoffman said, "but we couldn't retract free ones."

In one meeting, a product manager stood up and declared that LinkedIn should pivot to job listings and embrace its future as a rival to HotJobs.com or Monster.com. "Let's be like Monster.com, but cleaner," he argued.

Hoffman sat quietly while the room split into camps. Some agreed: job boards made money. Others felt that a pivot would betray the bigger vision of trust-based networking. Hoffman listened, then asked the entire team to pause and write down what they personally wanted LinkedIn to stand for in five years.

When they read their notes aloud, the word *trust* surfaced again and again. Job boards commoditized people; LinkedIn would empower them. That meeting crystallized their North Star. They would not be a job board. They would be a professional network. It also reinforced a bigger lesson: meetings must tackle existential questions head-on.

By prioritizing trust, the team decided that it would ban fake profiles. LinkedIn couldn't be a place where bots can spread memes and misinformation, like on Twitter (now X), which launched in 2006. It had to be trustworthy and transparent enough so that you could even incorporate a premium feature such as receiving a list of all the profiles who visited yours. That might seem creepy on Facebook, but it proved to be accepted as useful on LinkedIn.

The meetings that led to these decisions required participation of everyone. "If you don't speak up," Hoffman said, "you are considered to have been 100% in agreement. And you'll be, you know, lashed with a wet noodle if you speak up later. Why didn't you speak up at the time?"

When Facebook launched its public-facing platform in 2006 and became an instant nationwide sensation, a couple of product directors argued that this was it: "LinkedIn is doomed. We're going to be killed by Facebook." "I was like, okay, well, I'm really glad you are talking about this," Reid responded. But I and others argued that LinkedIn was different in fundamental ways, which we outlined for all to see:

- ◆ **Professional focus strategy.** Avert social media drawbacks by focusing on saving time, not spending time, and by maintaining civility as a safe place.
- ◆ **Three strikes and you're out.** Implement a baseball-inspired three-strike policy for violations, with some offenses receiving all three strikes simultaneously.

- ◆ **Account restriction philosophy.** It's very difficult to get restricted accounts unrestricted because violators showed they're not good network members.
- ◆ **Real identity requirement.** Having an aggressive approach to fake profile removal was one of earliest and most important policies. Fake profiles get tossed immediately.

As a result of these decisions, LinkedIn has largely avoided the problems of misinformation, fake profiles, and incivility that has plagued the other major social networks. "We proved that you could set up the kind of the network you want by establishing the terms of service," Hoffman says. "That meant that you could complain if someone even did relatively innocuous things like hitting on you. We established very low tolerance for incivility, insults, slander, and for posts that included misinformation."

This business model that prioritized trust over unrestrained growth meant that LinkedIn would expand at a much slower rate than Facebook or Twitter. Hoffman likens it to the tortoise and the hare. As the tortoise, LinkedIn would reach its goals, he believed, but it would take longer to get there.

Becoming the World's Largest Professional Network

By 2007, LinkedIn had hit critical mass. Ten million professionals had joined, new venture capital funding was flowing, and new employees arrived every week. Hoffman knew that as the company scaled, the meeting culture had to scale too or risk collapsing under bureaucracy. He worked with his executives to codify meeting norms that balanced speed with depth. Foremost among these principles were these standards for meetings:

- **An owner for every meeting.** Who circulates agendas in advance appoints a notetaker, and afterwards tracks actions and responsible parties.
- **Pre-reads are sacred.** No one walked into a decision meeting cold. Materials went out at least 24 hours in advance. If you hadn't read them, you didn't get to weigh in.
- **No spectators.** If you didn't have a role, you didn't sit in. Meetings weren't performances.
- **Start with wins and gratitude.** Kick off meetings by recognizing what has gone right and thank those responsible in order to keep morale and energy high—not just focus on what has gone wrong.
- **Disagree and commit.** Once a decision was made, debate ended. The whole team backed it, whether they had agreed initially or not.
- **Eliminate unnecessary meetings.** Regularly review schedules and be ruthless about cancelling recurring meetings that are no longer crucial.
- **No meeting days.** Work groups set a weekly day (e.g., Wednesday) when everyone can work uninterrupted. It doesn't mean you can't have a meeting, but it means none are scheduled.

These simple rules kept meetings focused and lean. As LinkedIn's headcount grew past 500, then 1,000, they added rituals to reinforce these norms. Weekly product reviews became a sacred fixture. Teams presented not just progress but also lessons learned. They celebrated failed tests that revealed user truths as much as features that scaled successfully. One product manager joked that LinkedIn's real product was not the profile page but the Thursday Product Review, where ideas got forged, challenged, and improved in real time.

Scaling the Meeting Culture

When Jeff Weiner joined as CEO in 2008, Hoffman had already stepped back into the role of executive chairman, and he continued to refine the meeting culture even further. The two men shared a belief that strategy without execution is hallucination, and execution requires alignment. Weiner brought with him a love for clear frameworks and crisp meetings. Together, they shaped an executive meeting cadence that has since become legendary in Silicon Valley.

Every Monday, the E-Team gathered for a three-hour block. It opened with personal check-ins, a ritual Hoffman had borrowed from his days at Apple. "If you don't know what's weighing on people personally," he'd say, "you don't understand how they'll show up professionally."

After that, the team turned to business: metrics, blockers, and strategic bets. Heated debates were encouraged, but everyone knew that personal attacks were not. One executive once said the culture made it impossible to hide behind politics: "If you disagreed, you'd better say it in the room. Otherwise, you lost your right to complain."

The nuts and bolts of meetings at LinkedIn were further codified. There were at least three different categories of meetings:

Weekly Business Reviews focus on metrics and performance. Each department (Sales, Product, Marketing, etc.) typically holds its own. Data dashboards (built in-house) are shared ahead of time so the meeting is about decisions, not just updates.

OKR Meetings are held quarterly to review objectives and key results. This includes leadership and cross-functional teams. The emphasis is on alignment and accountability.

1:1 Meetings. Managers are expected to have regular one-on-one meetings with direct reports. But special skip-level meetings, such as a vice president meeting with a product manager, are also encouraged to keep leadership accessible and connected to ground-level feedback.

In terms of the tools used in these meetings, LinkedIn set standards for slides and dashboards for data visualization. Certain material has to be circulated in advance of the meeting. If there is no agenda, there'd be no meeting. All meeting invites must include clear goals and an agenda. Starting with gratitude and wins helps build a culture of recognition and appreciation. There is a strict respect for time, with 25- or 50-minute meetings instead of full- or half-hour blocks. Meeting owners encourage punctuality and end early if possible. "In the room" decision-making became the norm. Decisions are ideally made in meetings, reducing long post-meeting threads.

To prioritize work-life balance, there was a family-first dinner policy. All employees are expected to go home for dinner with their families, then return online from 8:30 to 10:00 p.m. Monday–Thursday for any pickup meetings and interactions.

Meetings Are the Company Culture

As LinkedIn expanded globally, its meeting culture had ripple effects far beyond Silicon Valley. Satellite offices in Dublin, Bangalore, and São Paulo adopted the same principles: clarity, candor, and action. Around the world, Hoffman's meeting ethos was translated as have fewer meetings and make them meaningful. Don't meet just to share status; meet to make decisions. Push for action and clarity, not endless debate. Encourage transparency and bold thinking, even in disagreement. Don't let meetings slow down execution; they should *accelerate* it.

Hoffman would later describe LinkedIn's meeting culture as a "distributed operating system for trust." It enabled thousands of employees, spread across time zones and languages, to work toward a common mission without falling into the traps that kill big companies: endless committees, vague accountability, and hidden agendas.

Some of the company's biggest breakthroughs, like opening its application programming interface to developers, acquiring SlideShare, and rolling out LinkedIn Learning were born in rooms where junior engineers challenged assumptions and senior leaders actually listened.

When LinkedIn went public in 2011, its S-1 filing told a story of strong financials and huge growth. But the real story, Hoffman would say, was cultural. "A good product can make you successful," he wrote later. "A great culture makes you inevitable."

Years after stepping back from day-to-day operations, Hoffman reflected on what LinkedIn's meeting culture taught him about building enduring companies. On his podcast *Masters of Scale*, he often asks guests about how they run meetings and pushes them to think of meetings not as a cost, but as a core engine of scale.

These are a few of the lessons he distilled for founders and leaders everywhere:

- ◆ **Meetings are where trust compounds.** If people don't feel safe speaking up, they won't tell you when you're wrong. A culture that punishes bad news is flying blind.

- ◆ **Candor must be engineered.** It won't happen on its own. You must set rules, reward dissent, and model it as a leader.
- ◆ **Don't meet to update.** Meet to debate, decide, and unblock. Updates belong in dashboards and emails.
- ◆ **Smaller is stronger.** The fewer people in the room, the more honest the conversation. If you can't feed the team with two pizzas, as Amazon's Jeff Bezos famously said, the meeting is too big.
- ◆ **End with ownership.** A meeting with no next steps is just theater. Decisions must have a clear who, what, and by when.

In 2016, as Microsoft was completing its $26 billion acquisition of LinkedIn, the buyout agreement included an understanding that it would retain its independence and autonomy, which is underpinned by its strong meeting culture.

That's how Hoffman struck a deal with Microsoft CEO Satya Nadella that required LinkedIn to remain stand-alone rather than go through a forced integration. Still operating largely independently today, LinkedIn now connects over a billion professionals worldwide. Its value lies in connections, yet the connections that mattered most in its early days were the ones forged in war rooms and brainstorms, tense debates, and hammering out tough pivots.

Over the years, the primary revenue source has remained enterprise sales for recruiters and salespeople who are willing to pay a premium subscription fee for hundreds or even thousands of seats. Along with premium subscription fees from individual users, LinkedIn's revenue streams add up to about $12 billion per year.

Looking back, Hoffman believes the hare and tortoise analogy came true. Like the hare, other social networks are more boastful about their rapid growth. But like the tortoise, LinkedIn established a slower and steadier path to success. "For years and years," Hoffman says, "we were thought to be the most boring social network."

But for Hoffman, the meetings that made LinkedIn were not boring, and they weren't just interludes between "real work." The meetings *were* the real work, the crucibles where ideas were sharpened, where strategy turned into action, and where the fragile threads of early trust became the steel cables of a multi-billion-dollar company. In the end, LinkedIn's greatest innovations might not only be its web of professional connections but also its blueprint for how to gather people in a room and make every meeting matter.

PART II

Principles

CHAPTER 7

Transform Scheduling

When Scott Cook drew up his list of "meeting maladies" in the early years of Intuit, little did he know how prescient he'd be, as many of those maladies have metastasized at countless organizations over the years like cancers on company culture. The list has also expanded to now include dozens of reasons why meetings are slowly killing your company by wasting time and money and depressing morale.

In setting out to write this book, I decided to run surveys of people working at all levels in companies and to ask them to rank the most pervasive meeting maladies. The data tells a fascinating story of more than 20 such maladies. Most significantly, I noticed that the top five maladies all pertained to what happens *before* the meeting, which seems to doom what happens *during* the meeting.

Meetings are scheduled to run too long. That was the number one culprit, followed by maladies that stem from a lack of a clear agenda for the meeting that should be set in advance and circulated to participants as part of the invitation. The lack of a clear agenda with decisions that need to be made in the meeting explains the number two malady: "no clear decisions were made," followed by "we didn't need this meeting—it could have been an email or chat thread" and "people came unprepared" and "too much time spent on tangents versus top priorities." What these failures all have in common is that they could have been averted by putting extra effort or intelligence in setting up the meeting, which would determine whether the meeting was necessary.

Fix Meetings, Fix the Company

The mandate for changing your approach to meetings needs to come from the top. Shopify is a case in point. By the outbreak of COVID in 2020, the e-commerce giant had grown to 10,000 employees who were all now suddenly working remotely. Charged with managing and growing its network of more than two million online merchants, these workers went overboard in setting up Zoom calls and conferences.

One day in early 2021, Shopify's founding CEO Tobi Lütke checked his online calendar to find it chock-full of endless meetings. He decided to drill down into the analytics feature of his calendar and was alarmed by what he found. Apparently, his engineers, designers, and product managers were spending more time talking about work than doing it. The logs revealed hundreds of recurring meetings clogging schedules, many without agendas. Attendance lists swelled with people who didn't need to be there. Wednesday afternoons looked like a productivity dead zone of "quick syncs" that typically stretched on for an hour.

Lütke is a German-born software geek who moved to Ottawa, Canada, where he and Scott Lake started Shopify in 2006 to support their own online store that sold snowboards. By creating free programming tools and apps for merchants to get their online stores up and running, they grew into the world's biggest host of virtual storefronts. But growth created bottlenecks that were now slowing down the company.

Lütke saw the problem in engineering terms: meetings had become *muck* in the operating system of Shopify's culture. Just like bad code, they were gumming up everything.

His solution was as radical as it was simple. In one announcement from the CEO, Shopify canceled nearly all recurring meetings with more than two people, banned meetings on Wednesdays, and required that any new meeting include a clear agenda. "Meetings are a bug, not a feature," Lütke declared.

Employees were stunned. Some worried that without their weekly touchpoints, teams would drift out of sync. But within weeks, something unexpected happened. Projects started moving faster. Engineers had more uninterrupted hours for deep work. Decision-making accelerated. In an industry obsessed with velocity, Shopify had rediscovered a lost truth: to speed up, you sometimes must slow the meeting machine down and even disable it before putting it back together again.

After all, modern tech companies run on three core resources: talent, capital, and time. Of these, time is the most constrained. You can hire more people. You can raise more money. But you cannot add more hours to the day. And yet, time is squandered in meeting rooms—both physical and virtual—where little of value gets accomplished.

A recent Atlassian study found that the average knowledge worker spends *31 hours a month in unproductive meetings.* If you count the time it takes to schedule and prepare for these meetings, it seems that meetings kill about a week of work every month. For a 1,000-person tech firm, that's equivalent to paying 150 full-time employees to sit in rooms and discuss things that could be handled in a more efficient way.

Translating lost time and lost productivity into money is not always straightforward. Another recent study found that bad meetings cost employers approximately $25,000 per employee per year.

I believe the actual figure is much higher because bad or unnecessary meetings carry hidden costs beyond the wasted hours. They fragment attention, erode momentum, and sap energy and enthusiasm. Employees are forced to switch contexts, each transition imposing a cognitive tax. People lose the creative flow they need to solve complex problems. Product teams miss shipping deadlines because decisions that could have been made in 20 minutes are dragged across multiple 60-minute meetings.

More anecdotally, I've asked countless employees about their least favorite part of their workweek, and three complaints rise to the top, all related to meetings:

- **Too many meetings.** My schedule leaves no room for deep, focused work.
- **Meetings that run too long.** Discussions sprawl far beyond their usefulness.
- **No clear agenda or purpose.** People show up unclear on why they're there or what they're supposed to decide.

I kept noticing that these complaints tend to zero in on problems with scheduling. Each challenge can be solved—but not with piecemeal fixes. The companies that succeed treat meeting reform as a cultural overhaul, not a scheduling tweak, even though it might look that way at first.

Ban Meetings on Wednesdays

Founded in 2006 to create tools for managing workflow, the San Francisco software company Asana was also experiencing a productivity problem. The leadership team of the San Francisco–based company noticed that employees, especially engineers, were constantly in reactive mode, ping-ponging between Slack messages and meetings.

By the start of the pandemic, the workforce had grown to nearly 2,000 employees. The irony of a workflow company having workflow problems was simply too much to bear.

The team settled on a policy of No Meeting Wednesdays. The reason many companies pick Wednesday is simply because meetings on Mondays and Tuesdays should be sufficient to give everyone their marching orders in a typical workweek. By Wednesday, everyone should be heads down, with a deep focus on getting their work done, not continuing to chat about what they need to do.

As a result, the calendar on Wednesday is sacrosanct. There should be no recurring team syncs. No ad hoc check-ins. No one-on-ones. Just uninterrupted stretches for deep work. Ideally, you reach a frame of mind that has been dubbed *flow* by Mihaly Csikszentmihalyi, the Hungarian American psychologist who became known as the *father of flow* due to his many books and studies on this mental state.

In a work environment, flow refers to a state of deep focus and immersion in a task, where individuals are so engaged that they lose track of time and their sense of self-consciousness. It's a mental state characterized by intense concentration, creativity, enjoyment, and a feeling of being "in the zone." This state is often described as a merging of action and awareness, where challenges are met with a sense of mastery and effortlessness.

At both Shopify and Asana, the policy of No Meeting Wednesdays was not optional, but it stuck over time because so many employees reported a sense of flow. Senior leaders modeled it by blocking their own calendars and refusing meeting invites. Over time, Wednesday became the most productive day of the week at both companies.

Companies can, of course, choose any day of the week as a meeting-free zone. But Mondays are ideal for weekly kick-off meetings, and Fridays are wonderful for meetings that build camaraderie and send off everyone with good vibes for the weekend. That leaves the middle days as the best options, in my view.

So, I ran an online poll, asking the question: if your company could have one of Tuesday/Wednesday/Thursday as a meeting-free day, which one would you choose? When the responses came in, Wednesday won by a large margin, garnering 56% for the proverbial hump day, versus 33% for Tuesday, and 11% for Thursday. Due to the way a typical work week goes, I always recommend freeing up Wednesday as the day to let everyone focus heads down on getting their work done. And at least from this small sample, people seem to agree.

Cut a Quarter of Meetings Each Quarter

A good rule of thumb for transforming scheduling pertains to the meeting bloat that accumulates on the other days of the week. The idea was pioneered by Slack Technologies, which was founded in 2012 to develop a platform for internal company communications. Like Asana, Slack is a San Francisco–based workplace productivity company that has a low tolerance for wasting time and money.

Over its first eight years, Slack chat channels caught on, grew steadily, and became pervasive. Yet when the pandemic struck, and a new surge of demand materialized among those working at home, Slack's own workforce of 2,500 was suffering from the same malady as many other companies: too many meetings that were sucking up too much time and money, sapping the energy of its employees.

Slack's chief operating officer Cal Henderson compares meetings to salt: "Just enough salt makes the dish work; too much salt ruins it." He and the leadership team began encouraging work teams to cut 25% of their meetings each quarter.

To enforce it, Slack began to run calendar audits, in which recurring invites are challenged: Does this still serve a purpose? Could this be asynchronous? Can the attendee list be trimmed? If the answer to any is yes, the meeting is either trimmed down in time, reduced in size, or cut out entirely. When applied consistently, this audit can recover thousands of work hours per quarter.

By the middle of 2021, the company was running more efficiently at a time when Slack channels had become indispensable for so many teams around the world. At that time, Salesforce bought Slack for nearly $28 billion, one of the top five software acquisitions of all time.

The 50-Minute Hour

One of the drawbacks of scheduling meetings back-to-back is that participants have no chance to take a break or answer urgent emails. It's why Google defaults most internal meetings to 50 minutes instead of 60. That 10-minute buffer isn't just a break—it's a safeguard against scheduling a continuous meeting marathon. For the same reasons, quicker check-ins are encouraged to last 25 minutes instead of 30. A side benefit is that the reduced time forces focus and discourages tangents.

The Short, Strategic Stand-Up

Another leading software company that makes tools for improving team collaboration, Atlassian, was founded in 2002 by two college friends in Australia, Mike Cannon-Brookes and Scott Farquhar. Over its first 20 years, Atlassian grew to $5 billion in revenue and 12,000 employees. One of the ways leadership has kept both morale and productivity high is via the use of short, strategic stand-up meetings. When you're sitting, you can more easily drift off. A stand-up meeting signals that you'll be back to work in a jiffy.

That's why all Atlassian development teams use daily stand-ups where each person shares what they did yesterday, what they're doing today, and any blockers. Standing keeps energy high and discourages rambling. Most of these meetings wrap in under 15 minutes.

The Schedule Stopwatch

Time constraints such as these can serve as powerful motivators. These constraints aren't about micromanagement; rather, they're about protecting the most valuable resource in a tech company: uninterrupted work time.

It's why some of the most productive companies set calendar defaults to 15, 25, or 50 minutes instead of the typical half-hour and one-hour time slots. To enforce the best use of limited meeting time, appoint a timekeeper for each meeting. Or use visible timers in Zoom or the room. Ending the meeting early and giving people back some time is also a great way to reward people for having an effective meeting. End the meeting as soon as its purpose is met.

The Who, What, When, Why Rule

Every meeting needs to justify its existence. If a meeting isn't necessary, it should be cancelled before time is blocked out. At LinkedIn, Reid Hoffman pushed for a simple discipline: every meeting invite must answer four questions in writing:

- ◆ Who needs to be there?
- ◆ What is the desired outcome?
- ◆ When is the decision needed?
- ◆ Why is a meeting the best format?

If there are no answers, then there's no meeting.

To build this discipline into scheduling, every invite should include the meeting objective, topics to be discussed, time allocation, and assigning a decision owner. Including a link to the agenda in a shared document that participants can review beforehand is an essential way to help everyone come prepared. Attendees should feel free to decline any meeting without an agenda. When these kinds of rigors are applied before the meeting, the meeting itself becomes shorter and sharper.

Building a Meeting-Smart Culture

Yet policies alone don't shift behavior; culture does. The tech companies that have transformed their meeting habits embed these practices into their DNA:

Public metrics. Shopify shares internal "meeting debt" dashboards showing total hours spent in meetings per team. The visibility creates peer pressure to keep numbers low.

Leadership modeling. At Slack, executives cancel their own recurring meetings when they no longer serve a purpose, signaling to others that it's not only acceptable but expected.

Regular reviews. Atlassian holds quarterly retrospectives on meeting effectiveness, treating meetings like a product feature that needs iteration.

These cultural signals reinforce that meeting discipline is not a one-time project but an ongoing commitment. When meetings improve, everything improves. The gains ripple across the organization. This way, more deep work gets done. Shopify's purge freed up an estimated 150,000 hours in a year, equivalent to regaining dozens of full-time employees.

Faster decisions. Amazon's narrative memos cut circular debates and rehashing, accelerating product launches.

Higher morale. Asana's No Meeting Wednesdays increased engineering throughput by 23% and boosted employee satisfaction scores.

Better meetings also sharpen focus on the work that actually matters. Teams move faster because they're not constantly stopping to realign. And when alignment is needed, it happens with precision.

The Multiplier Effect of Smart Scheduling

On the first Wednesday after Shopify's 2021 meeting purge, Maya Gupta, a senior engineer, opened her calendar and stared at the blank expanse. No "quick syncs." No "brainstorm blocks." Just uninterrupted time. She dove into a tricky architecture problem that had been lingering for weeks. Without a looming meeting to interrupt her flow, she cracked it before lunch. By Friday, the solution was in testing. Multiply that by thousands of employees, and you begin to see why Tobi Lütke called the purge "the most productive code we've ever shipped."

In the end, fixing meetings isn't about making them shorter or fewer for their own sake. It's about reclaiming the most precious asset in any tech company: the time, focus, and creative energy of its people. Meetings should serve the work—not the other way around.

A Smart Scheduling Checklist

Based on these lessons, I created a checklist for these proven practices and put them into daily use at any kind of company. What follows is five overarching scheduling practices, along with the goal for each, and specific ways it can be reached.

- Reduce the Number of Meetings

    Goal: Free up time for deep work and faster execution.

    How: Run a calendar audit monthly. Cancel recurring meetings without a clear ongoing purpose. Consolidate overlapping topics into fewer meetings. Move updates to asynchronous formats (Slack posts, shared docs). Set meeting-free days (e.g., Asana's No Meeting Wednesdays). Identify Quarterly reduction targets (e.g., Slack's "Cut 25%" rule).

- Shorten Meeting Length

    Goal: Prevent meeting sprawl and protect focus time.

    How: Set shorter default durations of 15, 25, or 50 minutes (Google's "50-minute hour"). The timekeeper role: assign someone to monitor and call time. Stand-ups for quick syncs: standing meetings encourage brevity (Atlassian). End early: conclude once the objective is met—don't fill the time just because it's booked.

- Require a Clear Agenda and Purpose

    Goal: Ensure meetings are intentional and outcome-driven.

    How: Set an agenda gate: no agenda, no meeting. The agenda must include objective, topics, time allocation, decision owner. Circulate agendas in a shared doc before the meeting for asynchronous preparation. Use purpose prompts (LinkedIn's Who, What, When, Why rule). For high-stakes meetings, prepare a written narrative memo that is read in silence at the start of the meeting by all (Amazon).

- Build a Meeting-Smart Culture

    Goal: Make meeting discipline part of the company's DNA.

How: Track and publicly share meeting metrics (Shopify's dashboard). Leaders should model the behavior by canceling unnecessary meetings. Hold quarterly retrospectives on meeting effectiveness (Atlassian).

◆ Four Questions to Ask Before Every Meeting

Goal: Create a gate that every meeting must pass through.

How: Before scheduling a meeting, ask yourself, Is a meeting the only way to achieve this goal? What's the minimum group needed to make the decision? What's the smallest amount of time we can allocate? How will we know the meeting was successful?

CHAPTER 8

Energize Your Teams

Running a meeting is like being a conductor in an orchestra where you must balance the energy around the room. A little more timpani, a little less violin, a little more horn section. You move the energy around the way a conductor does at Symphony Hall. What I mean by that: if someone is talking too long, really droning on because they like the sound of their own voice, you interrupt them and switch it to someone else.

How to energize people in meetings is touched on previously in the book. But now it's worth taking time to dive deeper into the techniques that the best meeting cultures deploy to engage, motivate, and inspire their teams. Start with the smallest possible meeting. I mentioned how my sweet spot is the three-person meeting. The reason I like the small ones is you can control the dynamic better than with a larger meeting. While my personal favorite is the three-person meeting, I also like four- or five-person meetings, but I can also run meetings with 100 people or whatever the number is. Over the course of running 20,000 meetings in my career, I've done them every which way.

What matters most is the energy and keeping it high and moving. When someone doesn't talk for a while, you ask them a question; you try to get everyone participating as much as you can. It's also important if you're running the meeting to be a cheerleader. When someone says something amazing, reinforce it. Say, "Let's make sure we write that down." This shows others that you're validating smart contributions and the people who make them. But it's also important to be critical. If someone presents a bad idea, raise your concerns immediately, and ask questions to guide thinking. "Would that really work internationally, for an international audience?"

Whatever the question is, whatever concern you have, don't save it for later. You want to ask it as soon as possible so that you'll have time in the meeting to discuss it among the group. The main thing is to move the energy around the room, get everyone to participate, and shut down the people who are talking way too much. Highlight the people who have good ideas, but who might be shy and who might usually not talk at a bigger meeting, but if they have good ideas, you want them to talk.

Also make sure there's a high quality and diversity of opinion. You want young people to speak up as well as people with 20 years of experience. All genders, races, religions, and so on. You want to make sure that you're getting input from everyone around the room.

Especially new employees. You want them to speak up as soon as they join in their first meeting. I learned this from my own experience. After I sold my first company to Intuit in 1999, the purchasers felt that we needed to be indoctrinated into the company. Our team was working out of a rented warehouse in Arlington, Massachusetts, at $8 a square foot and I had 15 employees. The Intuit brass came out from California during indoctrination week—some human resources (HR) people and some information technology people—and they put in a $70,000 phone system.

My engineers were scratching their head just looking at it, going like, "I've never seen anything so expensive. All the computers together in our company didn't cost that." We bought used computers because we were frugal. And then they drop in a $70,000 phone system for a 15-person office. It was amazing to us.

The priority should have been not spending money on fancy equipment but energizing us as a team. They had HR teach us about Intuit's values and all that, but it was more like an information dump than a meeting. In response, I created something new that I called *reverse indoctrination*. When you acquire a company or hire a team or hire a person, you have a precious, short amount of time—one week to three weeks—where you can extract information from them before you program them to think like you do, to think like what I call *the borg*, short for a cyborg robot from *Star Trek* that controls all the humanoids.

I'm very much anti-borg and very much pro-individual. If you're good at hiring, and you bring talented people on board, you want their ideas. You literally just spent a month recruiting them. You think they're amazing. If they really are amazing, don't have them spending their first day training to think like you through indoctrination. Do this reverse indoctrination thing where they get them to speak up in meetings, especially during their first week. They may have a vision for their next phase of the company or at least the next phase of their career.

At Kayak, we built a team of more than 200 talented people before being acquired by Priceline, now Booking.com. Some weeks would have two or three new people. Sometimes we'd go a week without adding anyone new. We also had some involuntary turnover at Kayak. In those first 10 years, maybe three people quit out of engineering. A few people were fired if they didn't perform well with others, or if they had a toxic personality.

We had the No Assholes rule in effect. But we went beyond it for meetings. We called it the No Neutrals rule. We wanted everyone to be so pro-team that if someone was just a wallflower, they're sucking up the oxygen in the room. They're not really strengthening the team because they're not engaging with people. And we wanted everyone to engage with other people in the room. You couldn't be an asshole, as that results in negative energy, and you couldn't be neutral, as that results in no energy.

Making Meetings Joyful

High-energy meetings are often joyful in the sense that they're fun, evoke positive emotions, forge a sense of purpose, and you're doing something you desire. I believe that joy is an essential element of meeting culture. Yet joy can be subjective to each of us. How can you measure joy in a more objective way? What does a joyful meeting feel like?

Joy shouldn't be synonymous with fun activities, like make-your-own ice cream sundae after lunch. That's great to do occasionally, and people will say it was fun. But they didn't learn anything. They didn't change. Rather, a joyful meeting is one in which people participate, contribute, and learn.

One great way to accomplish this feeling of joy is to do exercises. Don't just talk to people for an hour. Give them a brief assignment that they can do on their own, in pairs, or in breakout groups. That's how they learn and connect with colleagues. That is my takeaway from Scott Cook's learn-by-doing philosophy. Creative problem-solving can be fun. Collaborating toward a common purpose boosts morale and motivation.

Establishing a joyful meeting environment is vital because we spend more time in our jobs than we spend with our kids or our spouses in a given workday. And for that reason alone, we need to make it fun and joyful. People perform better when they're happy and having fun.

Here's one simple metric for keeping tabs on how joyful your meetings are: What percentage did you initiate versus percentage of meetings initiated by another person? If you are only attending meetings scheduled by others, your soul will be sucked dry as you become a servant to other people's calendars who request you. Just by saying yes, you could end up attending several hours of other people's meetings every day for your entire career. That's a horrible way to exist.

Don't let all those meetings crowd out meetings that you want to lead. After all, meetings are often seen as tasks that must be completed. Sometimes, attending a meeting evokes a sense of obligation. Someone else scheduled it, and you are required to go, at the request of your boss or to serve another colleague's agenda. It's a nearly surefire way to lower the energy in the room.

By contrast, meetings that you initiate have greater potential to be joyful. It's why I believe that you should make sure that between two and four hours out of every eight hours of meetings are ones you initiate. What's your hot button topic? What's important to you? If you are driving that agenda, then you have a far greater chance of making the meeting joyful for you. It's a rough index: 25% to 50% of your meeting time should serve your needs, your desires, your agenda.

In my case, my calendar is color-coded. Blue meetings are my day job running my current startup or managing my other ventures. Yellow is nonprofit work. Green means self-improvement. Purple is friends and family. In a typical day, I spend the majority of my time in meetings. But if I could have two hours a day where the meeting was initiated by me, that means I'm getting my agenda done. That goes for all the colors on my calendar.

Whatever color, I approach meetings the same way. I always like to make a connection with people I'm meeting with, whether it's over something we have in common or establishing a common purpose. After all, whatever you are discussing will soon be forgotten, but what lasts is that bond you have with people. I believe wholeheartedly in that quote attributed to Maya Angelou: "People will forget what you said, people will forget what you did, but people will never forget how you made them feel."

In this sense, bringing a sense of joy and levity and compassion to your meetings transcends everything else. How would you like to be remembered after you're gone? It's a question that we should ask ourselves from time to time. I love this piece of folk wisdom that is said to have ancient origins: "They say you die twice. Once when you stop breathing, and a second time when somebody says your name for the last time." It reflects a human desire for remembrance and a fear of being forgotten. To me, it means you should think about the arc of your life and the journey you are on. Are you heading in the right direction? Will you be remembered for the positive ways you made people feel?

What both quotes tell us is we have a journey in our life and if we want to be remembered, we need to be strategic. And being strategic is that we are the average of the five people we spend the most amount of time with. Be selective whom you spend time with. Make sure you're spending time with people who will bring you along your journey and you in the right direction. And then the other thing is, as you look at your calendar, are you meeting with those people? Are you meeting with people who give you joy? Are you meeting with people who are great collaborators who can ideate and cocreate?

Make sure every day has joy in it. When you initiate a meeting, it's part of your journey, and if it's a meeting with those five people you want to spend time with, all the better.

A simple way to measure this is to know the average number of minutes a day you spend in meetings requested by other people versus meetings requested by yourself.

When a leader knows how to engage people, it's often said that the leader has charisma. This quality of charisma is often defined as charm or attractiveness that can inspire devotion in others. I take it as a compliment when people tell me I have charisma, and I believe it's something to which we should all aspire. Put more simply, if you have charisma, people will enjoy their time with you, and they will follow your lead.

One of the key ways to be charismatic is to be dynamic. In a meeting, it's imperative that you vary your tone of voice. Sometimes you talk fast, sometimes you talk slow, sometimes you talk loudly, sometimes you talk softly, sometimes you talk in paragraphs, other times you talk in phrases. Being dynamic is one of the best ways to energize a meeting.

Empowering Teams When They Meet

Sometimes, a new person can come up with something worth pursuing that could even change the trajectory of the company. Often, people come up with something unexpected. At Kayak, many individuals helped early on. Mike Bernardo was our lead iPhone Operating System engineer and the designer for the iPhone app. We jumped in as soon as Apple opened the App Store in 2007. Bernardo led our thinking there about what the platform could become. We had a series of meetings in which some people argued that the iPhone wouldn't be materially different from the web platform. Bernardo argued that it could be quite different.

I created a mobile platform team led by Bill O'Donnell (Billo) as chief architect and with Mike Bernardo leading the design. I told them they didn't need to build in all the features of the desktop Kayak. Just figure out what would look the best on an iPhone app. And even if the features work differently, we're still going to call it Kayak. But we want it to be your vision for this team about what makes a good travel app. And they did some things differently. They added some features that didn't exist on desktop Kayak. And there were some features on Kayak that they didn't do in the app. We really gave them the freedom to have this small five-person team innovating and adding new features every week. They ended up building a really good product. I think if I constrained them to say, make it look just like Kayak desktop, it would not have been as good a product.

And it was fast. The app worked at lightning speed, and it grew rapidly, reaching 50 million users within a few years. We put a lot of energy into speed. I remember buying yellow plastic stopwatches and handing them out to the performance team. I had about five engineers spread across the company I charged with making the app run faster. Since they had a yellow stopwatch on their desk, when people walked by and saw someone with a yellow stopwatch, it meant that's a performance person, pay attention to them, help them, don't get in their way.

I called it my Stopwatch Team. The performance guys on the iPhone team indeed figured out how to make it as fast as possible. They had free reign of the whole code base, so they didn't have to just stay isolated in their own code. Any problems or overlaps or intrusion or issues were worked out in a series of small team meetings.

If I saw a meeting with 10 people in it, I would intervene and start asking questions and throwing people out of meetings. That's why I came up with using a tally clicker like they do to estimate crowd sizes or take product inventory. I hung a tally clicker on every conference room doorknob to remind people of the small meeting rule.

Starting a Meeting with High Energy

Going back to the conductor who moves the energy of the room, this means you need to start on high energy and end on high energy. The problem that inevitably arises at the beginning of a meeting is that some people are two or three minutes late. Some companies are strict about showing up to every meeting on the precise starting minute. I don't believe in that. Some people need to show up two minutes late because they are finishing their preparation for the meeting. Or they can't find the Zoom link right away. It happens. When it does, it means there are other people sitting around for two minutes, twiddling their thumbs, and it can be awkward. Small talk ensues: How was your weekend? How's the weather today where you are? Where else are you up to today? All that stuff. Some people get really negative about the chitchat at the beginning of a Zoom meeting.

I disagree. I think it's useful as a way to tune people to each other, to find a way to connect about something that's not at work. I often like to open a meeting by talking about something fun. Especially because these days when a lot of meetings are remote, you don't get the water cooler time to talk with people about other stuff happening in their family or their house or whatever.

On Zoom meetings, you must artificially create those moments so people can connect on a human level, not just a work level. You don't want to spend too much time doing it. I like to spend two or three minutes at the beginning of a meeting just saying, "Hey, how'd that thing go?" It could be a work thing or a social thing. "How was that?" You just ask the question to someone, just to warm up and establish the energy of the room.

"Did you do anything fun this weekend?" I do that one a lot, just to sync people with each other, which I like doing. I like hearing about people's weekends. I like to know what they do outside of work and all that. But for a larger group meeting, I wouldn't do that. For a bigger group, it's helpful to focus on work. I might call out one person and say, "Hey, you went to that trade show yesterday. How was it?" Empower someone who actually wants to tell their colleagues about the trade show.

It should be something specific that gets the conversation flowing naturally. I started my career as an engineer and then ran engineering for a 1,000-person company. And then we hired a new CEO, and he put me in charge of marketing. And I'd never done marketing before. But as part of marketing, I had to do a lot of public speaking. And because I had an engineering background, and am a little bit nerdy and a little bit on the spectrum, it did not come natural for me. In fact, it was very difficult for me. And I developed this technique of starting a conversation naturally.

People coached me on a couple things, and from then on, I was able to start on a naturally high-energy note. One technique that I learned was if you're about to go on stage to do a presentation for 1,000 people or 10,000 people and you're nervous, if you just stand there by yourself, they turn the lights on, you start talking, your voice will crack sometimes because you're so nervous.

My technique for getting around that was I would chitchat with someone backstage, like a photographer. "Hey, tell me about your camera. How long have you had that? Is that the latest Nikon?" And you're just practicing your voice, to get it running, and then the light turns on, and you're already talking. It always works. You warm it up.

A meeting is like that, too. You do a warm-up. That gets the talking happening.

But I don't take too long doing it. Maybe like two or three minutes. I'll do funny things every now and then. At the beginning of the pandemic, people missed each other because they had been in an office, and suddenly we had to send everyone home. And so we'd start Zoom meetings with games. In Zoom, they have a plug-in where you could build in some games and you could play games against each other. We would do that every now and then as an icebreaker. Trivia games about music or movies or TV shows were our favorite.

Nowadays, there's an app store inside of Zoom, and there's different games you can play, including trivia games against each other. I don't do that anymore because now people are used to hybrid meetings. But at the beginning of the pandemic, we used to not only kick off our meetings with a game but sometimes we would schedule meetings just for playing games. Games are generally good for team building.

One woman at the company, Stacy Scott, had a weekly meeting of her customer service team. They called themselves the Wombats. When they had the Wombat meeting, she would have one question, just like two to three minutes. At the beginning of every meeting, she would ask someone to talk about something fun. If it was November, Stacy would ask, "What's your favorite Thanksgiving side dish?" And go around, for everyone to say, "stuffing, potato pie, cranberry sauce," whatever. She did that as a way to get everyone participating really quickly on something. And then she'd jump into business. I like that.

I often don't do that specifically, but I like the idea of starting the meeting with something friendly because we're not all just workers. We also are humans. We're parents, sisters, brothers, husbands, wives. I like starting with just a few short minutes of human, nonwork stuff.

Best Practices for Energetic Meetings

Yet when you walk through the halls of most companies, you'll hear the same groans: "Another meeting? Do we really need this one?" If they're not high energy, meetings can eat away at morale and productivity, rather than being the heartbeat of organizational alignment, especially if they stretch too long, involve too many people, and inspire little action. In the world of tech, where speed and clarity can make or break billion-dollar businesses, some companies have found a way to turn meetings from a dreaded time sink into the sharpest tool for innovation and smart execution.

Let's quickly step into four companies that have reimagined the way the energy of meetings flow: Amazon, Google, Netflix, and Zoom. Each reveals a different principle for how to make meetings not only effective but also inspirational. These are gatherings where people leave more energized than when they arrived.

As we learned about Amazon, meetings don't start with chatter, PowerPoint decks, or long-winded introductions. They start with silence. Attendees walk into the room, grab a printed, tightly written narrative, and spend the first 20 to 30 minutes reading it in silence. Only after everyone has absorbed the document does the real meeting begin.

The result is that meetings at Amazon aren't dominated by whoever talks loudest. They're fueled by ideas, clarity, and shared understanding. Leaders don't waste time "catching people up." Everyone starts from the same baseline.

This culture of disciplined preparation through clear, narrative writing instills respect for time. It also gives everyone, from junior analysts to senior executives, the same access to the argument. At Amazon, the most important voice in the room isn't the most senior; it's the best idea clearly expressed. So, if you want high-energy, effective meetings, don't settle for surface-level prep. Demand the kind of preparation that forces clarity before the meeting even starts.

At Google, the company famous for "20% time" and moonshot projects, the chaos of creative energy can quickly overwhelm an organization. That's why its meeting culture leans heavily on structure. At Google, no meeting happens without an agenda—shared in advance, linked in the calendar invite, and clear about purpose. The agenda doesn't just list topics; it defines decisions to be made. Without that clarity, the meeting doesn't happen.

Then there's the emphasis on data. Google's product reviews, for example, don't revolve around opinions or politics. They are based on dashboards, user metrics, A/B test results, and customer insights. It's not about who has the strongest personality; it's about what the evidence shows. This emphasis on rigor doesn't kill creativity but rather fuels it. When engineers or product managers present new ideas, they don't need to convince others with rhetoric. They show experiments, prototype performance, or customer reactions. Meetings at Google feel less like debates and more like collaborative investigations.

Perhaps most important, Google meetings are designed to be short and decisive. The company popularized the idea that the "default" length of a meeting should be 30 minutes, not an hour. That simple constraint keeps people focused. It's hard to waste time when you only have half an hour. Google's culture of structured, data-driven, agenda-based meetings keeps the company moving fast while ensuring decisions are informed by evidence rather than ego.

If Amazon is about discipline and Google about structure, Netflix is about candor. The company's culture document, famously shared online, makes one thing clear: honesty, even if it stings, is a gift. Meetings at Netflix embody this principle. Employees are expected to give blunt, unvarnished feedback in meetings. Sugarcoating wastes time. Silence is seen as withholding. The assumption is that everyone is operating in good faith, and therefore candor accelerates improvement.

Founding CEO Reed Hastings often emphasizes that the job of leaders is not to control decisions but to set context. In practice, that means Netflix meetings are less about top-down direction and more about equipping teams with the right information to make great calls. A product strategy meeting might involve a leader laying out competitive dynamics, financial realities, and lessons from past experiments but then leaving the decision to the team.

This approach creates an atmosphere where people feel empowered, not micromanaged. Meetings don't drain energy with endless approvals; they energize by putting responsibility in the hands of the people closest to the work.

Add to that Netflix's mantra of "freedom and responsibility," and meetings take on a sharper edge. If you're in the room, you're there because you have a role to play. You're expected to speak up, share your perspective, and take ownership. Passive attendance isn't tolerated. As a result, meetings at Netflix aren't about consensus. They're about candor, speed, and accountability. They inspire because people feel trusted, and trust fuels energy.

Finally, we turn to Zoom itself, the company whose technology powers millions of meetings worldwide.

The Silicon Valley-based company grew from 1,700 employees in 2019 to about 8,000 in the wake of the COVID pandemic, when Zoom suddenly became a household word. All along, Zoom has tried to model what great virtual meetings can look like. Zoom's internal culture emphasizes presence. Cameras on, distractions off. Meetings are shorter than average—25 or 50 minutes instead of 30 or 60—to allow for transition time. Leaders try to model good behaviors: muting when not speaking, calling on quieter voices, and making use of breakout rooms for deeper discussions.

Zoom also invests in training employees on how to run great virtual meetings. It's not assumed that people know how to facilitate across screens. Skills like managing group energy, using chat effectively, and designing clear follow-ups are explicitly taught.

Perhaps most important, Zoom practices what it preaches about balance. Eric Yuan, the founder, has spoken often about the risk of "Zoom fatigue." The company sets norms about not scheduling back-to-back virtual meetings and encourages asynchronous communication whenever possible. Meetings are for when real-time collaboration adds unique value, not by default. The result is a culture where meetings are not just functional but often energizing, even in a virtual format. Zoom demonstrates that the right norms, tools, and training can make virtual collaboration every bit as effective as in-person, sometimes more so.

Taken together, these four companies show us that great meeting cultures are not accidents. They are designed. They are intentional. And they reflect deeper values of the organization: Amazon's silence and narratives show the value of preparation and clarity. Google's agendas and data show the power of structure and evidence. Netflix's candor and context show how trust fuels speed and ownership.

Zoom's presence and training show how to design for energy in a virtual era. What unites them is the belief that meetings should not be routine. They should be events that matter, gatherings that spark ideas, align teams, and inspire action. And maybe that's the simplest lesson of all: the best meetings aren't about time spent. They're about energy gained.

How to End with High Energy

There is no better way for a meeting to create momentum than to end it with a burst of energy and a sense of purpose. At the end of each meeting, I summarize my major takeaways, which I flagged along the way in my notes during the meeting, usually in a Google document. I'll tell everyone what I'm most excited about. If it's a product road map meeting where we're talking about what's coming out next week and over the next month, I'll say, "I'm looking forward to these next steps or milestones that we're going to finally see this product feature doing X, Y, and Z."

I see this as a reliable rule: let people know what excited you most about the meeting. Tell them explicitly right at the end of the meeting. Touch on a couple of the action items, which will always be in the notes, but say it as well. The ones that are most exciting of all the action items are the ones that could change the direction of the product or the company the most.

I name those action items specifically and then say, "Okay, so Eliza, you're going to get us the new vertical industry analysis. Ashley, you're going to bring us a new marketing plan"—just make it clear that the meeting was an important hour or half hour.

There's work that needs to happen between the meetings, of course. So, make sure that at the end of the meeting you're talking about what we take from this meeting to propel us into the actual work. When you focus on the action items and what you're doing next, this naturally is going to be high energy because it's about action. You've already made the decisions. Now, it's about getting it done.

Taking notes in meetings has changed in a major way, given all the real-time transcription services that are based on LLMs which are at the heart of ChatGPT and other AI platforms. Every week, millions of meetings are transcribed by the built-in notetaker in Zoom or Google Meet, which uses its own AI-based Gemini tools. Millions of other meetings are joined by invited notetakers from Otter, Read.ai, Fireflies, Textalize, and Granola. They all do a nice job not only transcribing but also summarizing the main areas of discussion. However, this doesn't eliminate the need for human notetaking.

I've always been very observant of who can write the best meeting notes. Some people can synthesize what happens in a room really quickly. I always try to do this. I work on this myself, and I think I'm pretty good at it. In a one-hour meeting, some people will be taking 10 pages of notes. In the age of AI notetakers, this is no longer necessary. It's far more valuable for a human to synthesize, analyze, and flag what they think are the main highlights.

This is what I like to say: I think there's three things that came out of this meeting. How do I remember what the right three things were? We just talked for an hour, and different people can come away with different takeaways. It's something I practice. I make a written or a mental note and at the end of the meeting, I review my highlights with the team so we can come to a consensus about what to take back into our work. Stating the big three priorities is something AI does not do that well. These automatic notetakers often have 10 or more points, which flattens the meeting out, as if everything is an equal point. Prioritization is something a human can do much better than AI. After all, the human knows context that AI can miss. And this gets to ending a meeting on high energy. The energy is experienced within each individual and among all participants. It's a human thing. Although AI is extremely useful for meetings, it's up to humans to capture and impart a sense of mission and purpose that drives people to do their best work.

CHAPTER 9

Meeting Across Cultures

We have a team in Pakistan developing code for my latest startup company. As part of their work, these men and women hold meetings in which a discussion in English could suddenly switch into Urdu, the national language of Pakistan. When members of our team in Boston tune into these meetings over Zoom, the Pakistanis speak in English, as none of us knows a word of Urdu. The language switching happens before the Bostonians join and when we're not there. Yet we like to get meeting summaries and transcripts to track progress and performance, and when they speak to each other in Urdu, we cannot follow what's going on. They can go back and forth within a conversation or even mid-sentence. This is quite common among people who are fluent in two or more languages.

To help global teams navigate such occasions, we've built translation tools on top of one of the best AI-enabled, real-time transcription services. It does a better job recognizing different languages and dialects and translating them during the meeting itself, so everyone can follow along. It works well at handling multilingual conversations, better than any of the leading other transcribers. Suffice to say that the translation services available to anyone today are better than anything the United Nations General Assembly had in past decades. In a few seconds, you can not only see the words that were just spoken but you can also get a concise summary of the main points.

In today's hyper-connected economy, almost every large company operates across borders. A product brainstorm in San Francisco may include engineers in Bangalore, marketers in São Paulo, and designers in Berlin. Yet the global stage introduces hidden complexities that can sabotage even the most well-intentioned teams: not only linguistic preferences but cultural differences, too.

Misunderstandings multiply in real-time conversations. A casual American "sure" might be heard as a definitive "yes" in Japan, when it was only meant to keep the dialogue moving. Silence in a German meeting might be interpreted as disengagement by a Brazilian colleague, while in fact it signals deep reflection. Words matter. Gestures matter. The cadence of speech, pauses, even the willingness to disagree in front of senior leaders are all filtered through cultural lenses. Assumptions can mushroom into misunderstandings that can derail entire projects or corporate strategies.

How Different Cultures Can Shape Choices

Since human behavior is such a huge factor, meeting across cultures presents so many subtle challenges. Some people, like me, are naturally conflict-avoidant and must work to overcome that tendency. Other people are more willing to state what they feel directly. Still others are more prone to go along with a group's decision even if they have private reservations. When doing business globally, such behavior patterns are often ingrained in cultures.

Once you go beyond understanding accents, you are sometimes beset with other cultural traits. Some cultures are naturally more shy and reticent, while others are more aggressive and direct. This isn't just national cultures, but within nations. Cross culture doesn't just mean a cross country borders, it could also mean a cross regions. Team members in New York can be more blunt and abrasive, while those in California might be laid back and polite. When I worked for Intuit and ran the team in Boston, I found people in California to be more polite than people in Boston and New York. New Yorkers are known for being direct, whereas Californians tend to be more passive.

The phenomenon of cross-cultural understanding has been quantified in a fascinating set of studies with a design approved by Germany's Darmstadt University and Japan's Kobe University. The researchers begin by citing previous research that highlights a contradiction between the imperative of personal choice and the pressure to go along with a group. "The provision of choice and self-determination are crucial for autonomy and human motivation and make individuals happier and healthier," the authors begin. "On the other hand, evidence on social influence suggests that individuals tend to adjust themselves to the thoughts of the majority in a group pressure situation."

For their first study, researchers recruited a sample of about 100 Japanese businesspeople and 100 German businesspeople. Both groups were divided equally between men and women. The researchers designed a set of questions aimed at measuring the phenomenon of "vicarious choice," when others on your team make the choice for you, and you are faced with the prospect of following along. According to prior studies, Eastern cultures and Western cultures provide an entirely different context for such choices. "Against the backdrop of the greater emphasis on independence, the pursuit of personal choice is crucial for Westerners, as choice enables them to express their individual, autonomous selves through showing their preferences, attitudes, values, and feelings," the authors summarize. "On the other hand, Eastern cultures place greater emphasis on social adjustment and accommodation to others, while self-expression through choice is relatively unimportant."

The Japanese and German groups were asked to imagine three scenarios:

Scenario 1. You finished a big project at work and your colleagues, and you go to celebrate this success with a meal. At the restaurant, you find a menu, but one of your colleagues orders for the whole team without asking for individual preferences.

Scenario 2. You plan an event together with your coworkers, and there are many tasks to share. Someone needs to take care of the finances, someone needs to do advertising, someone needs to invite and take care of the guests, and someone needs to do the paperwork. One of your coworkers takes the lead and tells you and the others what to do without asking for individual preferences.

Scenario 3. You are in a meeting and your boss asks for feedback about a new policy that he introduced last week. One of your colleagues answers in detail, representing the whole team without asking individual opinions.

For all three scenarios, the researchers calculated the likelihood of the Japanese and German participants to accept the vicarious choice and demand personal choice. The results were stark: Japanese participants were about 30% more likely than German participants to accept choices by others on their behalf. Correspondingly, German participants were about 30% more likely than Japanese participants to demand that they get their own personal choice.

What the study confirmed is a phenomenon that many international businesspeople have experienced anecdotally for years. The results support the hypothesis that vicarious choice and perceived consensus is more accepted and more positively connoted in Japan as compared to Germany.

I never want to stereotype groups based on my own observations. Without appearing biased, the study enables me to express what I have found specifically with Germans and Japanese businesspeople. The Germans I deal with are direct, and I love that. And the Japanese I deal with are so polite, it's sometimes hard to know what they're thinking about.

The study puts it more eloquently and precisely:

This indicates that Westerners likely perceive vicarious choice as a threat to their rather independently oriented selves, thereby promoting reactance. However, the emphasis on interdependence would lead East Asians to avoid social rejection by meeting others' intentions and expectations. Hence, the mechanism behind cultural variation in choice seems to be related to the extent to which people are motivated to avoid social disapproval.

This may be deep psychological stuff. The study delves even deeper by also looking at the underlying cultural norms that give rise to such behavior patterns. Japan's culture is more consensus-based at all levels.

But I believe it is possible to simplify this insight—by designing meetings in which participants are primed beforehand. In other words, they are given a summary of such a study, and told something like this, "Please speak up! Express your choice! We know that culturally this may not be what you usually do, but please: we want everyone who has an opinion on a certain matter to say how they feel." You might not have to tell that to the Germans, but the Japanese may need a reminder.

At the same time, the Germans can receive a summary of the same study, and be primed before a series of meetings to be aware that they must listen carefully to others and not express a strong opinion if they are okay accepting other options, too. These are vital nudges, especially to prompt Germans ahead of time with the imperative that consensus matters, too. You might not have to tell that to the Japanese, but the Germans might need a reminder.

How Airbnb Develops Capabilities Across Cultures

Meeting across cultures is especially challenging when it comes to the discipline known as "learning and development" (L&D). L&D is the umbrella term for all initiatives that help employees grow, such as onboarding, technical training, and professional development.

Through my conversations with leaders such as Airbnb cofounder Nate Blecharczyk, I came to appreciate how effective cross-cultural meetings can serve as the centerpiece for a strong form of L&D, building diverse and inclusive work environments that extend across the globe. "We're a truly global company, with people all around the world, in all 24 time zones," Nate says. "That means we need to develop skills and capabilities in all those places."

Airbnb operates in 220 countries and territories, including some areas that are not yet recognized as official nations. Each area of the world has its own unique differences. Understanding them can determine success or failure. In 2015, for instance, when Airbnb aimed to extend its local property listings to China, its English brand name didn't translate at all. Meeting with local partners, Airbnb's leaders came up with a new Chinese brand, Aibiying (爱彼迎), which means "welcome each other with love." The aim was to better express Airbnb's mission in a way that felt familiar to the Chinese. Even basic terminology needed to be expressed differently. *Host* became *home partner* and *guest* became *short-term renter*. Terms like *private accommodation, luxury amenities* and *home sharing* were replaced by *cozy stay*, *comfortable home-style*, and *authentic local experience*.

This seemed to work for a while, but Airbnb by 2022 ended its presence in mainland China, removing all its local listings before shutting down the national website and app. The reason: stiff competition from local platforms along with the challenging regulatory environment. Airbnb's withdrawal from China highlights how high the stakes are for understanding cultural differences and why meetings are crucial for developing those skills and sensitivities. After all, there's stiff local competition and challenging regulatory environments all over the world.

When it comes to conducting better cross-cultural meetings, I see these as the big questions: How can you help your people in different countries learn from each other? How can you design multicultural meetings in a way that takes a broad range of expectations into account?

Stephanie Lynch, the manager of training programs at Airbnb, offers tips on her process for multicultural training and describes how her team measures the impact of learning through shared experience. Stephanie notes that those who focus on cross-cultural learning are called *ambassadors*, as they require diplomatic skills. For instance, some of these ambassadors specialize in fielding questions from hosts, who may have security concerns, as well as from guests, who might have questions about gaining entry to a booked property. "We're speaking different languages, and our ambassadors are living through the lens of their individual culture and identity," Stephanie explains in a post on 360learning, a global L&D platform. "There are so many different attributes that we have to think about that lead to learning most effectively."

Indeed, the way different cultures receive customer service and solve problems has so many nuances that it's important for local teams to meet and share their experiences with other local teams. All this multicultural training must apply equally for professionals working in offices and those working remotely at home. "We're structured around thinking about who are our learners," says Stephanie. "Where are they? What issues are they solving? And then we try to build the learning experiences that they need to help them through their journey." That leads us to a more generalized set of learnings that any company can put into practice.

Five Ways to Overcome Cultural Barriers

Achieving the right balance when meeting across cultures can make a huge difference to business success. If a false consensus, for instance, ripples through a decision-making process, you might make a bad or suboptimal choice as a team or a company.

To bring out lessons of best practices of meeting across cultures, let's look at five guidelines to build stronger, more resilient organizations by learning to overcome any kind of cultural barrier.

EMBRACE TECHNOLOGY TO CONNECT AND ENABLE TEAMS

Make active use of collaboration tools (e.g., Workspace, Meet, Slack) to keep global teams aligned. Stay tuned for new platforms yet to be introduced!

Such platforms can include one of more of the following:

- **Translation services.** Integrated tools can help bridge direct language barriers that can lead to miscommunication.
- **Virtual collaboration platforms.** Shared digital workspaces like Notion or Confluence centralize

information, ensuring alignment and transparency across different locations and time zones.

- **Overlapping work hours.** While accommodating various time zones, manage scheduling to find overlapping hours for real-time meetings and discussions.
- **Asynchronous communication.** Using tools for asynchronous updates respects flexible work schedules and prevents burnout from late-night meetings.

ESTABLISH CLEAR, INCLUSIVE COMMUNICATION NORMS

Clear guidelines are necessary to prevent misunderstandings and ensure all voices are heard.

- **Define communication etiquette.** Global teams need to set explicit rules for interactions, such as confirming understanding after key discussions and using simple, jargon-free language.
- **Build psychological safety.** In some cultures, employees may hesitate to speak up in meetings, which can be mistaken for disengagement. Leaders must proactively create a safe environment where everyone feels comfortable sharing ideas.
- **Encourage active listening and empathy.** Promote listening attentively to diverse perspectives and showing empathy for cultural differences. This is more than a courtesy; it's a critical skill for understanding context.

FOSTER CULTURAL INTELLIGENCE AND AWARENESS

This goes beyond simple communication and involves deeper training and understanding of cultural nuances.

- **Provide cultural sensitivity training.** Workshops and training programs can educate employees on diverse cultural norms and communication practices. This helps teams understand differences in work ethics, expectations, and politeness.

- **Create cultural ambassadors.** Designating individuals who can act as mediators to bridge cultural gaps can help facilitate communication and build understanding.
- **Offer informal learning opportunities.** Employee resource groups and cross-cultural mentoring programs can foster peer-to-peer learning and the sharing of diverse experiences.
- **Decentralize where appropriate.** For local markets, respecting and adapting to local cultures is essential. This can include localized marketing and strategic local partnerships.

CULTIVATE A CULTURE OF FLEXIBILITY AND ADAPTATION

The most successful global organizations are those that adapt, not just expect others to conform.

- **Recognize varying leadership styles.** Understand that expectations of leadership vary by culture. Some cultures expect a hierarchical approach, while others value egalitarianism.
- **Flexibility in policies.** This applies to corporate policies, communication styles, and even approaches to time management. Some cultures operate on linear time (strict deadlines), while others have a more flexible time approach.
- **Embrace diversity as a strength.** Instead of viewing different cultural perspectives as a hurdle, successful global teams leverage them as a catalyst for more innovative and comprehensive product solutions.

KEEP IN MIND THE CULTURAL CHALLENGES YOU ALWAYS NEED TO OVERCOME

These common barriers need to be addressed:

- **Geographic distance.** Physical separation can make it harder to build rapport and trust. Overcoming time zone challenges requires thoughtful scheduling and effective asynchronous tools.
- **Language differences.** While translation tools help, nuances and idioms can still be lost in translation. Clear communication and language support are crucial.
- **Differing work styles and ethics.** Cultural norms about punctuality, communication, and decision-making can lead to misunderstandings if not addressed proactively.

By following these five sets of guidelines, a company operating globally or even across regions of a country can transform cultural barriers into a source of strength and innovation, fostering inclusive and highly productive collaboration.

The companies that thrive don't erase differences. They surface them, honor them, and build structures that channel them into better outcomes. The lesson for global leaders: don't just design better meetings; also design them to account for cultural differences that could make meetings worse.

CHAPTER 10

Analyzing Meetings to Make Them Better

In survey after survey of executives and employees, a clear majority of respondents report that most meetings they attend are bad, if not terrible. Given all that's at stake, this is a crisis, as bad meetings go beyond wasting money to damaging company culture and productivity.

The reasons why meetings are bad can be wide ranging, starting with disappointment with your own performance. For instance, what if you are told that you put "uhm" before every sentence or "hmm" after what anyone else says? There may be problems with team dynamics: what if a series of meetings vital to charting your company's future gets dominated by one participant, while someone else barely speaks up. There may be a flaw in the strategy behind what your team is doing. Or a certain topic gets low levels of engagement from participants. Or a regularly scheduled meeting almost always seems like a total waste of time.

These meeting maladies and many others point to my favorite aspect of meeting culture: finding ways to improve it. Fortunately, most companies now have a rich dataset that they can mine for clues to take meetings to the next level of productivity and creativity: the transcripts. With the shift to more and more virtual meetings, automatic transcription services have become both ubiquitous and far more accurate than they once were. For in-person meetings, many conference rooms have built-in recording consoles. It's also easy to record it all on a phone and upload the voice file to your favorite cloud-based transcriber.

When it comes to analyzing meetings and taking action to improve them, we indeed have a rich set of tools at our disposal, ranging from old school notetaking to modern transcription to person-to-person feedback to an emerging set of AI tools that can present a meaningful report on a meeting that just ended moments ago.

Our current startup is focused on building a set of analytics off the transcripts. With LLMs, we can custom train software to spotlight strengths and weaknesses of any meeting. It gets even more interesting when scaling the technology across dozens or even hundreds of meetings that happen inside a company in an average month. If you can get a summary of the main points of the meeting in a couple seconds, imagine what can be done with the transcripts across an entire enterprise.

These what-if scenarios brought me to an epiphany: that what happens in your meetings could be your company's largest and most valuable dataset. There are so many use cases for this data that it would be impossible to cover them in a single chapter. But in the end, each employee and each enterprise can create their own ways to use this treasure trove of insight to improve their meeting culture and turn meetings from a mind sink into a critical factor for success.

Looking at trends across multiple meetings based on transcripts will be commonplace in the future. It's a win whenever you identify the discussion quality or the outcomes for just one meeting. But multiply that across all your meetings for hundreds or thousands of employees and get a broader picture of what's going on. Why shouldn't meetings be the largest dataset that a company has about their own activity? There's already crazy amounts of effort going into product analytics, marketing analytics, and the like. What about meeting analytics?

Some might worry about companies meddling in the conversations of their employees. But these aren't casual chats or off-the-record moments. The privacy of private conversations can still be protected. Rather, these are on-the-record company meetings, which are supposed to be as official as official business gets.

Few companies have a handle on what is happening in their own meetings. It's kind of a black box. In the future, individuals and companies will be able to decide how meetings get analyzed and how to respond to suggestions for making them better. Along with any permissions needed or opt-in requirements, these options should be available to organizations. It should be transparent about what is being recorded, what kind of analysis is happening, and how much control individuals have over their own meeting content.

The Benefits of Radical Transparency

Let's look at how meeting data has been used effectively in the past. Decades before LLMs and instant transcription services were available, the investment management firm Bridgewater Associates aimed to glean valuable intelligence by analyzing its meetings. Founded in 1975 by the now legendary investment guru Ray Dalio, Bridgewater embraced a set of business and life principles that he honed over the years as the firm grew into one of the world's most profitable hedge funds.

The centerpiece of Dalio's philosophy is embracing what he dubbed *radical transparency*. "Realize you have nothing to fear from knowing the truth," Dalio writes in *Principles: Life & Work*, his bestselling personal memoir and business manifesto. "Have integrity and demand it from others. Never say anything about someone you wouldn't say directly to them. Bring problems and weaknesses to the surface, to deal with them in an open way, for rapid learning, effective change, and more meaningful work and relationships."

In Bridgewater's early days, he notes, everyone knew each other, so being radically transparent was simple. People could attend the meetings they wanted to and communicate with each other directly, either formally or informally. But as the company grew, that became logistically impossible. Dalio required that virtually all meetings be recorded and made available to everyone, with rare exceptions such as discussions of personal health. When you turned the lights on in a conference room, the recording started and everyone was aware that whatever they said would become available inside the company.

At first, Dalio sent these tapes of management meetings unedited to every employee, but that was way too time-consuming to digest. He had a team edit the tapes to isolate the most important debates, instances of clear decision-making, and other teachable moments, to create case studies used for training. Over time, the meeting highlights became part of a bootcamp for all new employees as well as ongoing training for everyone else.

The Wilton, Connecticut, company expanded beyond 1,000 employees and eventually exceeded $100 billion in assets under management, taking its place as one of the world's largest hedge funds. By the time Dalio retired in 2017, he had codified and left behind a set of 10 ground rules for effective meetings based on his conclusions from analyzing thousands of meetings over the years:

On meeting leadership: "If it is your meeting to run, manage the conversation. If it is not your meeting to run, follow the lead of the person who is running the meeting."

On why meetings go wrong: "There are many reasons why meetings go poorly, but frequently it is because of a lack of clarity about the topic or the level at which things are being discussed."

On purpose and accountability: "Every meeting should be aimed at achieving someone's goals; that person is the one responsible for the meeting. . . . Meetings without someone clearly responsible run a high risk of being directionless and unproductive."

On meeting format: "If your goal is to have people with different opinions work through their differences to try to get closer to what is true and what to do about it (open-minded debate), you will run your meeting differently than if its goal is to educate."

On groupthink versus independence: "The worst way to pick people is based on whether their conclusions align with yours. Groupthink (people not asserting independent views) and solo-think (people being unreceptive to the thoughts of others) are both dangerous."

On logic over emotion: "Remain calm and analytical at all times; it is more difficult to shut down a logical exchange than an emotional one."

On staying focused: "Topic slip is random drifting from topic to topic without achieving completion on any of them."

On interruptions: "The two-minute rule specifies that you have to give someone an uninterrupted two minutes to explain their thinking before jumping in with your own. This ensures that everyone has time to fully crystallize and communicate their thoughts without worrying they will be misunderstood or drowned out by a louder voice."

On demanding understanding: "Recognize that it's your responsibility to make sense of things and don't move on until you do."

On finishing discussions: "Conversations that fail to reach completion are a waste of time."

I would love to have Ray Dalio on my shoulder as I shape meeting culture, given the wisdom he and Bridgewater collected by recording and analyzing meetings over decades. Ray was operating before the days when AI could be deployed to train itself on an entire company based on this kind of rich dataset. In building such tools, we need to be careful and lay down some ground rules, something that every leader must address.

Using an AI as Your Meeting Coach

Above all, we need to respect people as individuals. That means giving them personal options to benefit from the use of meeting analysis. The paradigm that I like best is that AI in meetings can take on the role of a coach.

The best coaches will report confidentially to each individual in the meeting and not report up the ladder to upper management. If you are talking too much in meetings. If you are talking too little. If you are talking too loudly. If you appear disengaged. If you're saying too many "ums." If you're speaking too fast. If you swear too often. If you speak in a predictable and boring monotone, or if you vary your tone of voice and come across as more dynamic and interesting. Do you use humor effectively, or do you come across as humorless? You as an individual should know all this and more about your own performance. Coaches should tell you. They shouldn't report this personal feedback to anyone else.

But an entirely different category, what I call *meeting meta analysis*, can and should be available to everyone in the company, including upper management. Did the meeting include a quality discussion? Was there a structure to the meeting that followed the agenda? Was the meeting even worth having in the first place?

Some companies will want its leaders to be able to see in general how people are doing with meetings. This might include scorecards for individuals. For instance, Laura's meetings have been rated highly effective, but Paul gets a lower score. If so, Paul can use the AI tools to coach him. But it shouldn't drill down deeper than this metadata or overall scores.

After all, it would be creepy if the AI said to the CEO, "Hey, I've been watching Paul and his meetings. He talks about random stuff for the first 10 minutes. And he doesn't talk about the agenda until 10 minutes in." But it would be okay to see whether Paul's meetings are rated highly or not. And then the CEO or the vice president of human resources can go to you or your team and say, "You guys haven't had high-rated meetings. Let's talk about how we can be more effective and to make sure you understand the AI tools, how they can help you, and to see if you want to sit in on meetings with people who have rated the highest and see if someone wants to sit in with you in your meetings."

This way, employees see it as more of a personal coach, only reporting up general ratings of the meetings. This is a legitimate concern of a CEO or any manager. A company's meetings are official business, and they are costly, given that employees are getting paid to participate as part of their job. So, the company has a legitimate right, within reason, to have ground rules for its meetings and a desire to have productive meetings. To make sure that meetings follow a logical flow, that key discussions aren't derailed, that decisions are reached, there's been alignment on action steps. Is a team making progress on its stated goals, or are they stuck rehashing the same issues over and over?

Or managers could use these AI tools to gather general points of intelligence about what is happening inside the company. For instance, in terms of topics of discussion, ask, "What's hot? And what's not?" Managers could even use their meeting intelligence to ask questions to guide their own decisions. If you have a product idea or a marketing idea, you can easily search the thousands of past conversations and see every insight of anyone who's ever talked about something related to that in the past. That's just one specific use case. Every company will have their own preferences, needs, and desires that can be served by their set of meeting analysis and summaries.

Yet there's no question that many people have anxiety and worries over AI and how it will infiltrate their lives. That's precisely why there must be built-in limits on the use of AI for meeting analysis that prioritizes respect for the individual.

My view is that AI is going to get so good that executives won't be able to resist the advantages. They're going to tell their people that you must use this. It's going to make you a better sales rep, for instance. Let's say there's a company that has 20 sales reps, and let's say the top 5 sales reps by revenue are using AI as a coach. The other 15 reps are going to wonder why those five guys are making way more money than they are, wondering what they are doing differently.

I believe that AI as a meeting coach has incredible upside potential. If used in a targeted way like this, it will require a set of rigorous rules to make sure it's used productively, responsibly, and doesn't cause anxiety. It should all lead back to human-centered principles that were defined by the best meeting cultures.

In the end, I expect the most popular use of these sophisticated tools will be for giving people their time back. The most common complaint about meetings is that they waste their time. If so, more meetings should be cancelled or shortened so you can have more time to get your work time, or just to take a break and get outside to walk your dog.

What Makes a Business Meeting Good or Bad?

Recently, my startup team conducted an online survey via LinkedIn that asked respondents two major open-ended questions: First, what makes a good meeting? Second, what is your biggest pain point as it relates to meetings? Everyone was also given a chance to give other feedback and observations. I've organized a few insightful responses in the following table.

What makes a good meeting?	What is your biggest pain point as it relates to meetings?	Other feedback (optional)
Engagement, humor, and some mistakes	Scheduling, monotonous topics, ego creep	Obviously, a lot of the times the meeting can just be an email, but when you make it more human and tangible it becomes more memorable and has a bigger impact on the team.
Getting something out of it, having a clear agenda	Unclear agendas, last-minute scheduling (e.g., when offline for the night and scheduling for 7 a.m.)	More meetings could easily be asynchronous. However, I have noticed it's harder to have clear conversations in tools like Slack when working with international teams due to the limitations of English and how we as Americans speak it versus other countries.
Big ideas that are actionable and room for varied perspectives	Too long, could've it been an email?	Loss of purpose? Generally, we have so many clients who want regular meetings to keep things moving, but it ends up being most of the time we show up to a meeting with all of our ducks in a row and they have not moved the needle on anything to support the work from the previous meeting.

(continued)

(continued)

What makes a good meeting?	What is your biggest pain point as it relates to meetings?	Other feedback (optional)
People engaging in a specific obstacle	Too big and too many just providing updates	Meetings are often "proof of performance," which rarely solves problems but can create job security.
Agenda + Leader + Short	Too long; too many people included; too often back-to-back and no time for context switching; ineffective room video/audio equipment; too many people multitasking on email or slack instead of paying attention	Former startup instituted 25-minute/50-minute meetings—that was great! You could get a glass of water or return an email between meetings.

Finally, we took all the survey responses and fed them into ChatGPT for analysis of the two questions. First, here is the distillation of the top five reasons why some meetings are good, along with specific quotes:

1. **Clear Purpose and Agenda**
   - A well-defined goal and agenda set the tone.
   - Attendees know *why* they're there and *what* needs to be accomplished.
   - Example phrasing from your notes: "clear purpose," "clear goals," "three questions," "meeting objective."
2. **Brevity and Efficiency**
   - Meetings should be as short as possible, ideally under 30 minutes.
   - Time is respected—people prefer brief, productive sessions over long, meandering ones.
   - Phrases used: "short and to the point," "briefness," "short, productive."

3. Prepared and Relevant Participants

- Only include those who are essential to the topic at hand.
- Participants should be ready, engaged, and ideally have done a pre-read or prep work.
- Cited multiple times: "prepared attendees," "relevant decision-makers," "right minds in the room."

4. Defined Outcomes and Action Items

- Meetings should end with decisions, ownership, or specific next steps.
- Without this, it's just a conversation.
- Key terms: "clear action items," "calls to action," "getting actual work done."

5. Engagement and Facilitation

- Strong moderation keeps things on track.
- Candid, inclusive discussion is encouraged, but off-topic tangents are managed.
- Phrases used: "active engagement," "facilitated discussion," "personal connection," "radical candor."

Following is the distillation of the top five pain points, including sample quotes.

1. Too Many and Too Long

- Overwhelming number of meetings in a week
- Meetings frequently running too long (often 1.5–2 hours)
- Standing/recurring meetings that feel unnecessary or redundant
- Comments: "Too many and take too long." "There's too many of them." "Long (1.5–2 hour) recurring meetings . . ."

2. Lack of Clear Agenda or Purpose

- Meetings starting without a defined goal or structure
- No clarity on what's being discussed or expected
- Comments: "No agenda, no chairperson, length." "Walking into meeting with no idea what the meeting is going to be about." "Not having a clear agenda . . . please be very clear."

3. Irrelevance to Attendees

- Inviting people who don't need to be there
- Meeting content not applying to everyone in the room
- Comments: "Only applies to 20% of the people in attendance." "Too many people invited that are not participating or providing value." "Not all in attendance need/or want to be concerned . . ."

4. Lack of Outcomes or Follow-Through

- No decisions being made
- No action items or ownership being assigned
- Comments: "Leaving the meeting without action items/ownership." "Meeting that ends without any actionable steps."

5. Poor Facilitation and Participation

- Off-topic tangents and hijacked agendas
- Dominating voices or people speaking to self-serve
- Comments: "People who like to hear themselves talk." "Off-topic hypotheticals that drag on." "People who blather on or hijack the agenda."

As it turns out, most meetings are pretty bad, according to surveys like this. Employees dislike over half of the meetings they must attend. It's why I believe there's a pressing need to study meeting transcripts and to coach each meeting host on how they can run better meetings, and to coach participants on how they can perform better.

The coaching must be kept confidential. Only the meeting host can see their coaching; we do not report up to the bosses of each meeting host. We never want to become Big Brother. We could show each host where they lost people in a meeting, where people got bored or stopped paying attention. We could coach them on things like talking speed, filler words, and so on. These are things that you'd have to otherwise go to weeks of Toastmaster meetings to learn.

Security and privacy are paramount. We believe meeting analysis software should be SOC 2 compliant. This is a set of standards for an organization, often a service provider, that handles customer data to demonstrate through an independent audit that it has implemented strong controls based on the Trust Services Criteria to safeguard data and systems. This framework from the American Institute of Certified Public Accountants assesses an organization's security, availability, processing integrity, confidentiality, and privacy to ensure customer data is managed responsibly.

That means data must be kept encrypted on secure servers. And each meeting participant should have the power to state their document retention policy (which data should be deleted how often) an easy ability to wipe all your company data off the servers in case you decide to end the service.

Given these safeguards, I believe we can help companies reduce cost by learning which 10-person meetings should be 5-person meetings, which hour-long meetings should be half an hour, which weekly meetings should be monthly, and which meetings should be canceled outright.

We strongly encourage companies to choose one day of the week with no regularly scheduled meetings—we default to Wednesday, but your site administrator can choose another day. We're not saying it will be impossible to schedule on that day, but a smart scheduler can steer around it in most cases.

The big goal is to improve what happens outside of meetings as well. Companies can and should increase focus time, which must be protected, especially for the creatives (engineers, marketers, designers, writers, etc.) so they have time to get "in flow." It has been well documented that creatives can produce work at 10× the speed if given ample time outside of meetings.

CHAPTER 11

Decision Points and Action Steps

What happens after a meeting is just as vital as the meeting itself, sometimes even more so. Since executing team decisions and following up on action items are the meat and potatoes of a team's performance, we need to outline principles on how that is best done. Part of the trick is to be a cheerleader for good ideas that come up during the meeting and say something like, "Susie, that was amazing." It's why I always aim to end the meeting on high energy by reviewing that we decided these three things, A, B, and C, and we have these two most important action items, 1 and 2.

Sure, an AI summary can do that too, but I believe you should do it verbally.

Then in between meetings, it's all about checking up on the action steps. Remind team members that these are decisions and action items generated excitement in the room. You're not performing these action items just to fill out an extra two hours a day. You're doing it because your colleagues are energized by these next steps and are depending on you to get it done.

An example of a great meeting and follow-up is from a Monday morning team meeting about a year into the starting up of Kayak. We had an engineer, Julie Melbin, who on the weekends was a race car driver. Julie raced competitively all over the East Coast. This one Monday, I asked, "How was your weekend?" She said she had a great race in Connecticut, coming in second place. I asked, jokingly, "Where'd you book your hotel?" Julie replied that it was on another travel site. I was surprised. "Why didn't you use Kayak?" She said, "Because there's no hotels close to the racetrack that are on Kayak." I got mad, and we discussed whether it was possible for this to never happen to any Kayak user. The team agreed that it was a great goal, but was it achievable?

In the wake of that meeting, I sent a follow-up email to the team, with the subject: Every Hotel on Earth. From now on, I declared, we must work to make sure that every hotel on earth must be on Kayak. At the time, that was more than 700,000 known hotels, plus an uncounted number of unknown ones. I said that I didn't care if a hotel pays us or not, but they must be part of our selection. The action item thereafter became known by its acronym EHOE. Inside Kayak, it was an action item that coined a new word.

We ended up achieving that goal within a year. When you are searching on Kayak where to stay, you can expect EHOE. Even the tiny little ones. We did it by crowdsourcing. We let anyone using the site tell us about a hotel. Let's say they were in the Greek islands, and they're walking around and decided to stay an extra day and they needed a new place to stay. They see a little sign saying room for rent. We said, "Tell us about it. We'll put it on Kayak." And so, our customers would tell us about every hotel. We made it kind of a game. Can you find a hotel that's not on Kayak? In retrospect, I wish we had done marketing about it. We never marketed EHOE, but I wish we did. I wish we told people we were giving away a thousand dollars a week to a randomly selected customer who sends us the name and location of a hotel that's not on Kayak.

As it turned out, our EHOE capability was highly valued when we were acquired by Priceline, now Booking.com. Being a booking engine for the "long tail" of any hotel in the world was a key part of the company's business model and value proposition. All of that came out of our Monday morning meeting when I asked Julie about her weekend.

When you summarize top decisions and action items, that team now has marching orders for the week. But what about in-between meetings? How do people stay posted and connected? Business chat tools such as Slack were created precisely for these kinds of group conversation, as are features of Microsoft Teams and Google. I'm not the best person to talk about Slack because I don't like it, although a lot of other people do.

Rather, I like to keep teams posted on decision points, action items, and follow-ups via email threads, and Gmail is especially good at that, although most email services provide a threaded view of a conversation. In this way, email threads are content-rich, whereas Slack can be ephemeral, with a constantly flowing stream of short comments.

I like follow-ups that express clarity of thought about action items as well as an argument you might be making. Think about why Amazon created the six-page narrative, not a half-page memo. If there was a meeting in which a big decision was made, email threads can keep track in richer detail of the conversation that follows through on the decision or the action point. There are 500 million people who use Gmail, and the reason I and many others like it is because it's fast and it can track a substantial conversation that happens over time. Email also enables a team leader to delegate something easily by forwarding a note or thread to someone who may not have been in the meeting.

These days, I get about 300 non-spam emails a day, and I send about 120. That means I receive about one non-spam email a minute. Here's how I deal with all that email traffic. When you get an email, scan it, and immediately do one of the following four things. My trick for remembering these four things is this alliteration: DDDD, for delete, do, delegate, and defer.

- **Delete or archive it.** You can probably delete more emails than you think, especially if it's outside the purview of your job or your meeting topics and especially if you're not the only person on the To/CC line. You may have the urge to reply with something witty, but you won't be able to keep your inbox to 10 relevant items at a time if you comment on every email. My reason for keeping it to 10 is that it appears in one iPhone screen on Gmail, and an email is way more likely to be forgotten once it drops to a second, third, or fourth screen. In Gmail, and I never actually "delete" email; instead, I archive it, using the keyboard shortcuts of *k* or *]*.

◆ **Do something about it, immediately.** If a colleague or friend asks you and only you for the phone number of someone else, look it up then, and send it to them. It will take you less total time to do this now than to save it and do it later. And you will do a better job helping your colleague.

◆ **Delegate, forwarding it if appropriate, to as few people as possible, ideally to only one person.** If you send it to more than one person, each one will wonder if they are supposed to do something with it or not. If you do forward something as an FYI to read, please take the time to put in an intro sentence saying why you think this is interesting.

◆ **Defer.** Worst case, hold on to it for later action. For Gmail, I use the Star feature to mark something for future action. But try as hard as you can to keep only 10 messages in my inbox. If you ever get more than 10, prune it so you can do one of the other *D*s on each message if possible.

I don't recommend creating folders. Using an email client with blazingly fast search, such as Gmail, you may be surprised how fast you can find any email without having to use folders (or labels). Folders are old-school for email software that did not have instant search.

The idea is to be as productive and methodical as possible when it comes to following up on decisions and following through on action points. With email threads, there's less of a chance that things will slip through the cracks as short messages scroll by in a chat window. Instead, there is a thoughtful, ongoing record of actions taken by the team. Then, by the time next Monday's team meeting rolls around, you can start on a high-energy note, by reviewing the progress made over the past week, updates on your action items, keeping momentum going.

How to Build Culture Change That Sticks

Often, a meeting can seem full of energy and inspiration, and you might expect those in attendance to carry that energy and inspiration back into their work. Yet nothing changes, and the meeting seems to have had little to no practical impact. This is particularly problematic when it comes to large meetings, especially an expensive, company-wide off-site with a big agenda, all aimed at building a culture of engaged employees.

During its first quarter-century, Intuit mastered team meetings, but founder and executive committee chairman Scott Cook is not one to feel satisfied, and he's always looking to build new capabilities. The most impactful way to do that, he believed, was to stage a major event. "I'm referring to the big, company-wide meeting, like when you get your top 100 or more executives together," he says. "And these things in companies typically happen once a year, sometimes more frequently. Typically, the CEO has some agenda, they're trying to drive some change in behavior across the organization, a change in belief or a change in behavior."

Cook tells a story of one such effort to drive culture change throughout the entire company. In 2007, Intuit kicked off a major initiative called Design for Delight to teach the organization the fundamentals of design thinking, lifting some lessons from Apple's success with the iPhone and other companies that transformed the user experience through intuitive design. A full-day meeting with the company's top 400 people were convened with sessions that featured great presentations with lots of visually stunning materials. The aim was to train design coaches throughout the company, and there seemed to be a huge burst of energy at the time.

But over the coming months and years, not a lot changed or came out of this big push or any other company-wide initiative kicked off in big meetings. "You could safely say we had lost our mojo," Cook reflects. "You could see it in the way decisions were made; you could see it in some of the success patterns of initiatives and not why they succeeded or failed, not the fact that they succeeded or failed, but why." The company seemed to be drifting, coasting, resting on its laurels.

By 2014, Cook set out to study the culture more deeply, looking at the actions and behaviors of people up and down the organization. He kept a list of what the organization did right and what was going wrong, with special scrutiny on why big meetings like that one didn't lead to lasting improvements or change. One conclusion: the company was trying to do too many things, spreading itself too thin over too many business franchises. "So, we stopped doing a bunch of things, and we sold off five divisions and product lines including one of the largest and our oldest, Quicken, the original business of the company—we sold it off. We also stopped all major innovation investment in our non-cloud platforms."

Next, Cook studied pockets of strength inside the company. "If you're going to change a company, I believe that you've got to have some evidence of success inside that same company. You just can't use other guys' stories, because people won't believe you if it's just Amazon or Apple doing it." One particular group inside Intuit had a major new product success. "We dove in, to try and understand what went right, and the big lesson, if I had to put a headline on all of it, it's that people *learn by doing*, not by talking or watching."

Learning by Doing for All

Looking back on those large meetings, Cook noticed that they centered on beautifully constructed PowerPoint presentations that everyone praised as magnificent and got top scores in all the feedback surveys. "But the thing I observed over time was when people go back to their office, they have the same email inbox, the same Slack, the same deliverables, the same schedule of meetings, the same team members who weren't at the meeting. And what would happen? Everyone would fall back into their pre-existing habits. Nothing would change."

The meetings weren't meaningful because it didn't change behavior. As Cook tells it, employees rated the entertainment value highly. But that doesn't drive change. You've still got your deliverables that you've committed to and those didn't change. The meetings were passive, like watching a TV show.

Curiously, there was one company-wide meeting in which a guest speaker from the Stanford Business School led the group in an exercise. He only showed three slides briefly, and then he led an exercise in which you had to divide into pairs, one person acting out the role of the designer and the other was the customer. The designer had to interview the customer. Based on the interview, the designer had to design something and show it to the customer.

The 40-minute exercise was just a small part of a long day dominated by PowerPoint presentations from the stage. But over the next week, Cook talked to many people who were in the audience and asked them, "So, what was your takeaway?" He found that five out of six takeaways were from the exercise, from that activity, not from the rest of the six hours. "It was from the exercise," he says. "That's what people remembered. And that changed my life forever. I've learned that adults do not learn by listening. They don't learn really by watching. They learn by doing. And if you want people doing different behaviors, you need to get them to do that different behavior."

Building on that epiphany, Cook collaborated with CEO Brad Smith to assign topics to executives that were largely new to them, out of their box, so to speak. Roles, titles, assignments, and people had changed as well, as it's the habits of Intuit's people that were often the barriers to change, according to Cook. Intuit swapped some business unit leaders, taking the same leader but putting them in charge of a different division just to lubricate good new thinking. Intuit also replaced a couple other leaders.

The reconfigured leadership team of 25 executives was then divided into three teams before being immersed in the new discovery process.

The mission: you had to personally research and engage in one focused topic for a few months, and then come back and present your research to the rest of the leadership team. For instance, you had to go to China, to study how personal finance is managed by families, and report back. Or understand what AI can bring to finance and report back. Understand young people and how they interact with computing; not just college students or high school, but kids in middle school growing up with smartphones.

The idea was to involve the leaders personally in the discovery process. They weren't allowed to delegate their activities, although many of them wanted to assign it to their team. They had to do it themselves, which means they had to be on the plane to China, for example, for that project.

In all cases, the leaders were changed by their experience, often in profound ways that could affect the company. But it wasn't enough that one leader did a project and reported back. Intuit expanded the concept into Learn by Doing for Everyone. This was based in part on the classic case of the General Motors executives who in the 1970s went to Japan to study the Toyota production system and why it still didn't penetrate US auto manufacturers for so long afterwards, even when GM put a Toyota-like process in their system. The key insight: if you send one guy out to see the new process and that guy gets all excited and comes back and tries to teach the other 10,000, it never works. You've got to take the whole group.

So instead of holding big company-wide meetings with fabulous presentations, Cook and Smith had everybody engage in direct learning and hands-on actions. Teams of two people went out to call on customers, meet them at work, and follow them home to see how they set up their personal finances. "This was not learning-by-lecture," Cook says. The old joke in college is that a lecture is the fastest way to transfer information from the professor's notes to the students' notes without going through the brains of either.

By contrast, this was a series of hands-on experiments to drive new ideas for innovation across the company. Everyone had to partake in the process from the beginning, understanding the customer problem all the way through to designing an experiment to run, and asking questions all along the way to learn what is happening and why. The meetings inside Intuit centered on designing experiments and asking the right questions, then going out to do it.

When Culture Change Leads to Growth

While innovation like this takes time to pay off, Intuit indeed introduced a slew of new products and entire business units over the coming years. The success of the learning-by-doing culture change was reflected in revenue growth, profits, and the previously stagnant stock price, which then skyrocketed by nearly 10× from 2014 to 2022.

The takeaway lesson for those designing meeting culture is profound. As Cook sees it, the chance is low that someone is going to leave a one-way presentation-driven meeting and go back to the office and do the behavior you want. "You need to get them to do that behavior now, in the meeting itself." Whereas the big design seminar in 2007 had little lasting impact, an event staged in 2017 aimed at retraining the entire company in design thinking was a smashing success. And it was because the meetings were centered on hands-on activities and direct exercises performed in pairs and small groups.

That concept of learning by doing "totally rocked my world," Cook says. "And now when I participate in a meeting, I start with this question: what's the behavior we're going to get people do that we want them to do and how do we get them to do that while we're together?"

It's a lesson that has been taught and learned by people over centuries. It's the concept of muscle memory. You can't just state it. You've got to do it. People must perform and practice the things that you want truly learned and remembered.

This is what changes the post-meeting environment in the office. If there's a behavior change you want, and you're going to have a meeting to try to do it, you also have to change the office environment when people return so they go back to something that's different to prompt the new behavior. What will be different next Monday morning?

Yet even though this lesson of learning by doing in meetings led to a company-wide resurgence, it's not a process that ever ends. "I would say this needs constant attention," Cook concludes. "I wouldn't claim a victory or a sudden turnaround or anything. It's about constancy, that you always need to refresh, remind, and reinforce behaviors and behavior change."

In the end, there is no end. Everything you've ever put into practice about running better meetings can be unlearned by an organization. People need continual reminders and reinforcements, and every new person needs to become an integral part of meeting culture from day one. Over time, great meetings themselves aren't enough. People learn by doing, not listening, or watching. At Intuit, the transformative experience that led to Scott Cook's epiphany was just one 40-minute interactive exercise during a day-long series of presentations.

After all, behavior change after a typical meeting is minimal when people return to normal work. To drive change, you must modify the office environment on returning in some way. It's critical to have participants practice desired behaviors not just during meetings but between them. Meeting effectiveness should be measured not by entertainment value but by lasting behavior change, through the breaking of old habits and the development of new ones.

CHAPTER 12

Scaling Meeting Culture

Scaling up meeting culture doesn't mean having giant meetings. It means having effective meetings across the entire enterprise. The way I've done most things at scale when I've managed large teams is by remembering to do two things. First, I redundantly talk about the change I'm trying to make. I go on about it multiple times. The teams are hearing from me the same message over and over again. Reinforcement works.

The second thing is I pick cultural leaders inside the company. Ideally, it's the vice presidents (VPs), but it might be a director or anyone who is seen as a leader. Someone who can deliver the religion, the mission, the mandate, and infuse it with purpose. This way, people will hear these key messages in two ways. They'll hear it from me over and over because I'm redundant in communicating anything that requires culture change. And then they'll see it in action when they're in meetings with the other cultural leaders.

At big companies, the overall culture changes and evolves over time. Intuit's early era was defined by coach-style leadership and discipline. During the next era, in the years I was there, I was told by Scott Cook and others that I had a significant effect on the meeting culture. After I left Intuit, the company went through a reinvention and a rejuvenation of the culture.

At Kayak, elements of the culture we created in the early years persisted over time. The meeting culture still is largely informed by the practices we put in place in the first decade. They still aim for small meetings, for instance.

I went back to Kayak in summer 2025 and consulted with them for a couple hours a week as requested by my cofounder, Steve Hafner, who was trying to make some changes there and he wanted me to help him. What I found was that it's become a more careful place as opposed to a groundbreaking place. For our first several years, people just broke stuff all the time as they tried new ideas one after another, in rapid fashion. "Let's do this, let's try that." That trial-and-error style worked very well for us.

But now, the scale of Kayak is hard to believe. There have been more than 160 billion travel searches on the website and the app over the years, according to Kayak's chief scientist. With so much scale, any company naturally starts being much more careful.

It's why a strong meeting culture is so vital to maintain as a company grows. I can think of no better example of how that happened than the story of how Amazon.com built and scaled its Amazon Web Services (AWS) technology business. Cultivated by Jeff Bezos, the culture that formed and grew in Seattle in the 1990s and early 2000s was so specifically designed and maintained that it wasn't clear whether it could be replicated and scaled anywhere else. Certainly, nobody had ever tried to do it three time zones and 3,000 miles away.

Cultivating Meeting Culture Across the Country

Back in 2012, Amazon's culture was so secretive that Wayne Duso wasn't told what the job was that he was interviewing for. Duso told me the story of how he was recruited from his leadership position at EMC in Hopkinton, Massachusetts, where he had worked for 18 years. The world's top supplier of data storage and digital infrastructure, EMC itself would soon merge with Dell to form the world's largest privately held tech company, and there would be lots of turmoil and turnover. But at the time, Duso wasn't looking to leave, and everything about his interviews at Amazon was top secret.

"I was recruited into AWS by Alyssa Henry, who was VP of storage services. She was one of the best leaders and managers I've come across, with incredible analytical capability. After a couple interviews, she said that I had to fly out to Seattle to meet Andy. I'm like, "Who is Andy, and do I need to fly out again?" And she says, "Well, he runs the place. That's it. He runs the place."

Turns out, Andy was Andy Jassy, who started his career shadowing Jeff Bezos but still was little known outside of Amazon. Jassy had written and presented the original six-page narrative with the vision of building and selling a set of cloud computing services to any company willing to jettison its own data centers and computer rooms, and thereby take the leap into a world where everything would happen on secure servers that somehow operated in the sky. Jassy would soon be named the CEO of AWS, which at the time accounted for less than 2% of Amazon's revenue. By 2022, just a decade later, AWS would end up generating literally all of Amazon's profits, as the e-commerce business was still often operating at a slight loss. But all that would have been unimaginable back in 2012.

"So, I go out to Seattle to meet Andy, and he asks me a bunch of questions," Duso says. "At the end of the interview, he closes his little brown engineering notebook and he says, 'Why should I let you open Boston?' Turns out, Amazon had selected Boston as the place where it wanted to transplant and scale its culture from just a handful of programmers to becoming a second software development headquarters that might one day have tens of thousands of employees."

"Is that on the table?" Duso asked, genuinely surprised. "It wasn't a part of the interview, it wasn't part of anything. And Andy goes, 'Yeah, it's on the table, but you've got to come and live in Seattle for a while. We've got to get to know you first, and you've got to get to know us.'"

That's how Duso was hired to build a system that came to be called the Amazon Elastic File System. "They said, we're trying to build this, but 'we don't yet know how, and we need someone who can figure it out,'" Duso recalls. One thing that was clear, though, was that Amazon needed to increase headcount outside of Seattle, and Boston was deemed as the best place to build what would become known as one of the most valuable businesses in history, as Amazon's market value rose from about $100 billion in 2012 to $1.7 trillion 10 years later.

The job offer happened and was accepted so quickly that when Wayne arrived at his general orientation session in Seattle and was handed out a laminated version of Amazon's leadership principles, he'd never seen them before. "The orientation sessions were small at that point, maybe 30 people in a room," Wayne recalls. "And there's this young man sitting next to me, an engineer hired out of college. When I read the principles, I go, 'Wow, this is amazing.' And the kid looks at me with the most disdain I'd ever seen on anyone's face. He probably studied his ass off, read them over and over, memorized every word. He goes, 'This is the first time you've seen them?' I said, 'Yeah.' He goes, 'How in the hell did you get the job?' And I go, 'I don't know, but I do love the leadership principles.'"

During his months of living in Seattle and spending 12 or more hours every day in the building, Duso became acclimated to the way the culture operates. His title, Director and General Manager of Storage Services, didn't attempt to capture a key element of his job. He came to realize that his most important role would not be as a software team leader or even for having a knack for whom to hire for what position. Rather, he says "stewarding the culture was my most critical role." He calls a company's culture "the fabric that weaves all of the disparate pieces together," and says that a big part of that is what happens in meetings and how they're run.

Duso's indoctrination at Amazon was awkward at times, as he took on the role of a sponge, absorbing everything, while hardly ever speaking in meetings.

> I paid attention carefully for the first three to six months, sitting in on every leadership meeting to understand how meetings were run, what they cared about, what questions Andy and the other leaders were asking. In fact, at one point, about three months in, I heard through the grapevine that Andy had asked my leader, who was Alyssa, "Why the hell doesn't Wayne ever talk?"

The truth was that Wayne was intimidated by the talent in the room. "I was afraid to talk because everybody knew everything," he says.

> It was the smartest group of people I had ever been around. Andy knew everybody's business better than they knew their own business. It seemed logistically impossible, but he did it anyway. So, I made it a point over the course of time to know my business. I went to every meeting knowing that if I don't know my business better than everybody else in that room, I'm failing.

What Duso absorbed about Amazon's meeting culture "is very straightforward," as he tells it. "You don't have meetings just to have meetings. You don't walk into a meeting with a traditional memo and PowerPoint. Every meeting is set up with a specific outcome in mind, and all of this is so ingrained in the culture." The name of the meeting will make the objective clear—whether it's a status review or a decision that needs to be made.

And every meeting that is set up comes with "a doc," meaning a well-crafted narrative up to six pages, and that's a strict limit. "Always, always a doc," Duso says. "If you walk into a room, and there's no doc, you have every right to walk out. You can have a 1,000 pages of back-up information in an appendix, but no one is required to read the appendix. You can have a one-pager, you can have a half-pager. As long as you make the point of the meeting clear in the doc, by stating whatever outcome you want to come out of it.

Importing and Scaling the Culture

After spending a few months immersed in Seattle, it was time for Duso to write his own doc, detailing the software's architecture as well as the plan for establishing the AWS development team in Boston. He describes the crafting of a doc as part art, part science, and as a skill that takes practice. "That first doc took 31 iterations over two months," he recalls. The doc needed to be read carefully by Andy and his leadership team, which included Alyssa. "No pressure," he jokes. "But I couldn't hire anyone until I got the doc approved."

In the narrative, Duso requested an initial team of 12 developers as the right number to get AWS in Boston going. And Andy said, "That's great, you can have five."

I said, "Okay, five is good, too."

Despite all the learning of disciplines practiced at Amazon, someone in Duso's shoes might still have believed this: "I know the EMC culture even better, because I was there for every kind of situation over 18 years, and it's how engineers in Boston work. Boston people might reject certain Amazon practices, by simply saying, 'That's Seattle, we're not going to do that here.'"

"If I had let that happen, we would have failed within a half a year, maybe a year tops. It absolutely would not have worked."

Duso began in Boston by hiring five engineers and moving the team into a Regus rental office by the waterfront in Boston's Seaport. The team quickly outgrew the space and moved to occupy half of a floor in the Cambridge at 101 Main Street in Kendall Square. That would make it easier to recruit from MIT, and the vibe there was entrepreneurial, as most of the other spaces were occupied by venture-backed startups.

Instinctively, Duso knew that he had to infuse this outpost with Amazon's culture, and to do it completely. "Being harmonically aligned with the culture is very, very important," he says. "If the vibrations of the culture and your vibrations match, life is going to be pretty good. If there's no harmonics, it becomes very difficult to operate."

Tasked with building a cloud-native file system that would form the unifying basis for AWS, Duso was asked to launch it in six months. It ended up taking two and half years. The challenge was that Duso was charged with building all AWS software "directly on top of the iron." That meant creating software native to this cloud-based environment.

This was more difficult than the alternative, which was to cobble together existing pieces of software native to other platforms, or by acquiring startups or repurposing code originally created for a different environment. It was understood that Microsoft was taking something akin to that approach for its development of what became its Azure cloud, a massive project led by a rising executive named Satya Nadella.

That put Amazon into direct competition with its Seattle neighbor for the first time. Historically, Microsoft has always preferred a modular architecture in which different hardware and software from different companies and computing environments can be integrated into a complete system. That was how the Windows ecosystem has always operated. The advantage is that development can be completed more quickly, products can be rolled out faster, and bugs can be fixed over time. But the drawback is that there can be problems with security, performance, and reliability along the way.

By contrast, Apple has always taken the opposite approach, creating a unified, completely internally designed system, built from scratch. That is how the Macintosh ecosystem has always operated and how Apple was approaching the iTunes ecosystem as well as its iCloud, which would be more consumer facing. To win against Microsoft in the business hosting world, Amazon decided to embrace Apple's ethos. So perhaps it was no surprise that the first three AWS services that had been developed in Seattle also took years longer than imagined.

The intense rivalry reinforced why the AWS team needed to move out from Seattle. The two big tech companies in town were often hiring from the same pool, and the secrets behind Amazon's juggernaut against its crosstown rival could better be kept in Boston. The stakes couldn't be higher, evidenced by how the cloud leader at each company would ascend to the role of CEO, with Satya Nadella replacing Steve Ballmer at Microsoft, and Andy Jassy replacing Jeff Bezos at Amazon. All along the way, each of these companies "built in line with their culture," Duso adds.

At Amazon, taking the extra time to "build native to the cloud" was in sync with the underlying culture of doing things in the prescribed way. That meant not only the way

Amazon conducted meetings but also the entire set of 16 leadership principles, such as customer obsession, invention, learning, high standards, bias for action, and responsibility for broad impact. One of the key principles mandates how one leader must be charged with ownership of a project, a task, or a subtask. This became critical for enabling growth of the team, to dozens, hundreds, and eventually thousands of employees. "After the third year," Duso says, "I felt as though I could start handing some of the reins to different people for different pieces."

From there, AWS in Boston experienced exponential results, growing Amazon's cloud offerings from a handful of services to over 300 a decade later. With Target's e-commerce platform as one of its first major customers, AWS was growing in demand at dozens of major companies and institutions per month that were moving their computing operations from local data centers into the cloud. That increased the pressure on hiring. Duso imported Amazon's guidelines, under which a successful one-day recruitment event was defined as attracting 75 prospects, with 25 moving to an extensive interview process, and resulting in hiring 5 new team members.

Every one of these recruits got indoctrinated into the Amazon culture, even though it originated 3,000 miles away. That meant learning how to write and read docs, and how to attend meetings where the first 20 minutes or so was spent in silence reflecting on one of these narratives and making notes to discuss it in depth. This seemed academic, but for recruits fresh out of MIT, it was in sync with how learning happened. "You end up studying a lot," Duso says. Many of these developers became managers and leaders in their own right and remain at the company today.

Taking an Epic Leap

The AWS team ended up outgrowing its Kendall Square location, and by 2018 moved into a larger headquarters on Melcher Street in the Seaport district, into a yellow brick building perched on the Fort Point channel waters. The open-office floorplan was built out with design elements that reinforced Amazon's culture. Instead of walls, reported the *Boston Business Journal*, the interior is divided by giant orange or yellow shipping containers emblazoned with some of Amazon's guiding principles: Bias for Action, Think Big, Innovation in Motion, Have Backbone: Disagree and Commit.

While 350 employees moved in, the space could accommodate up to 900. Despite the larger scale, each floor was designed for small meetings, with group sitting areas for three or four people facing a whiteboard. For remote meetings with Seattle colleagues, cozy phone rooms were equipped with video-conferencing screens.

A conscious effort was made to infuse every space with the company culture. Each floor of the office was themed with a different mode of transportation that an Amazon package takes, beginning with a fulfillment center on the first-floor lobby. That center features a wall full of shipping labels to and from some of Amazon's first employees. On the train-themed fourth floor, a wall featured a railroad crossing sign, model trains, and fun facts about Boston's railroad history. A community feel was also essential. With a theme of home, the sixth-floor space featured a library area, café, and a "backyard space" for group events.

Yet even this new facility wouldn't be able to contain the growth, as Amazon's AWS team in Boston eventually expanded to 4,500 as part of more than 20,000 employees in the Boston area, including warehouse and shipping personnel for the core e-commerce business. Not long after leaving the company in 2024, Duso reflected back on all of this growth and cultural cultivation, including developing entry-level engineers into managers, supporting sustainable growth and continual innovation.

"It's funny," he says, "now we talk about 2012 as the old days." In terms of technology, that was indeed an eon ago. As Wayne puts it,

Anyone like us who has been at this for a while has had a career spanning Four Epics. Number one was the Personal Computer Epic, which focused on desktop software and lasted from roughly 1980 to the mid-1990s. Then came the Web Epic, which was built on a client-server model of computing and stretched through 2010. That was supplanted by the Cloud Epic, which enabled mobile computing based around smartphones and apps. In 2022, the public launch of ChatGPT heralded the current AI Epic.

"If you think about your career in these phases of technology," Wayne concludes, "this is my fourth epic. That's the way it is now for a lot of people. Most of us can't even fathom it. For me, it's exciting." He forecasts that the AI Epic will last about as long as the others, 15 to 20 years. Next up, by about 2040, is the Quantum Epic, he expects, when quantum computers combine atomic precision with uncanny intuition to do things scarcely imagined by science fiction.

Yet as much as the technology advances, the human element must remain the same at its core. That means the culture, with meetings at its center. "Looking back on when I brought all of that here, I became that leader," Duso says.

I became the leader that people were watching in the room. Did I know that would happen? No, not as much as I came to realize. And in fact, when I left, people asked me, "Why are you leaving? You are

Amazon. You are AWS. You breathe this place." And
I said, "You do now, too. Like, you don't need me to
breathe this place. You guys are breathing it, too."

To that, I say, "Wow." My final thought is that all this
technological change, all this growth that technology has
enabled, all these jobs that have been created, all of it comes
down to whether you can establish a foundation, that that
foundation is the human institution of the meeting. And so
I ask you, dear reader, to think about the best meeting you
had in the last week and then think about the worst one. And
how would you like it if you had only great meetings in a
given week and no terrible meetings? That's a future that I can
imagine, and I think it's worth working toward.

Conclusion: Takeaways That Inspired Supercal

Those who have known me for a long time often have the same reaction when I tell them I'm writing a book about meetings. Several former colleagues reacted this way: "You could have done that 10 or 20 years ago!" I've long been called a "stickler for meetings," which is someone who insists on adhering to punctuality in meetings and values structure and efficiency, making sure meetings follow an agenda and have clear objectives and ground rules. To all that, I plead guilty.

But it's gone way beyond that. While researching and putting together this book, it's grown into an obsession with making meetings both more impactful and more joyful. Over the course of participating in perhaps 30,000 meetings, for all kinds of objectives, across organizations large and small, I've gleaned and internalized a set of takeaways for creating better meetings.

When it comes to scheduling, aim for fewer, shorter, and smaller meetings. Start on time. Have an agenda, one that points toward making decisions.

The person who runs the meeting needs to act like a symphonic conductor and move the energy around the room, getting input from everyone. Get new and junior people to talk first.

Have a process for moving off-topic items to a "parking lot" to be addressed after the meeting versus taking the time of the meeting with a focused agenda.

195

The secretary plays a vital role, as they take live notes, usually in a Google document with all attendees having comment access. Not a transcription of everything that is said. That would be boring and best left for AI. Rather, it's the main points of the meeting. I still believe that a good secretary is better than great AI at summarizing main points. Have the secretary maintain a decision log, writing down all decisions made in the meeting. The secretary can also point out when a discussion on a certain point is taking too long and can suggest that the meeting move on to the next topic.

If someone doesn't talk in a regularly scheduled series of meetings, they should not attend anymore, unless it's an informational broadcast meeting.

Be aware that men interrupt women more than women interrupt men. Fix this.

If your company is focused on customers (as most companies are), consider opening some meetings with a customer support leader briefly recounting a recent and noteworthy customer interaction. Keep an empty chair in the room to represent the customer.

Bonding and having fun should be priorities. Consider opening some meetings with a question of the day when you want some bonding to break the ice. If Thanksgiving is coming up, have everyone name their favorite side dish. If you're meeting on Monday after the Super Bowl, ask people what they felt were the best and worst ads.

Good meetings have conflict. This will cause people to pay attention. When someone says "let's take this argument offline," they are sometimes being conflict-avoidant. Those are often the very issues we should discuss in the meeting.

Meetings should have action items whenever possible. There are two goals of every action meeting: (1) make decisions quickly and (2) improve relationships with everyone in the room.

Have someone on a laptop that can tap into live generative AI research. But bring it into the discussions only when AI has something relevant to offer.

Consider using the DACI model, clarifying roles of each attendee or each person in an organization as it relates to a project that will be discussed in a meeting:

- Driver—the one person driving the project
- Approvers—a small list, ideally the two to three people who must approve decisions
- Consulted—we really want their input; should still be kind of small
- Informed—a larger group who receives an email update of the meeting

Stage interactive activities such as taking a minute of silence to write down thoughts or suggestions. Or have the activities take place in breakout groups or pairs during the meeting. Tap into experiences that happen between meetings. Activities and breakout groups are both vital and based on a key insight: adults learn by doing, not listening, or watching. That's a key insight from the best mentor anyone could ask for, Scott Cook. Here's another from him: meeting effectiveness should be measured by behavior change, not entertainment value.

End meetings early whenever you can. End each meeting with higher energy than it started. Constant attention needed to refresh and reinforce desired behaviors. In this sense, the art and science of making meetings better never ends.

For this next chapter in my career of building companies, I've been inspired by this set of takeaways and the many insights to launch a new startup called Supercal, the work-life intelligence company. Much of the Supercal platform was inspired by the many insights on meetings found in this book and by the many interviews conducted with people for research on the book.

There are two halves to the Supercal product. The first half of Supercal is a fast and free scheduling tool that takes on entrenched services such as Calendly. With Supercal, your meetings are set up in seconds, with no more long email threads—all done with the assistance of AI. Supercal-scheduled meetings happen sooner than a human-organized meeting. Supercal meetings also protect your free time for deep work. Smart, AI-based rescheduling of low-priority meetings happens in the background. Supercal works with Google Calendar, Microsoft Outlook, and Apple Calendar.

While finishing up this book, I launched the first half of Supercal, which was noticed by *The Boston Globe*. What caught the attention of *The Globe*, *TechCrunch*, and other media outlets is this leapfrogging of Calendly, which charges $12 per month. By offering a free service that does much more, Supercal immediately attracted thousands of users who have given us overwhelmingly positive feedback on its ability to read everyone's calendars, find a time that works for all, then book the meeting and reply to an email thread with the invite.

Supercal lets you sync up to six of your calendars, so you can keep work, personal, and other schedules in one place. It offers eight different meeting types, including 15-minute, 30-minute, and 60-minute slots, as well as a VIP meeting type that provides full access to your calendar for important situations. There are also breakfast, lunch, coffee, and dinner meeting types. In the future, these meeting types will feature an OpenTable integration that will enable you to book a meeting at a restaurant or coffee shop.

But it's the second half of Supercal where the most powerful value is found, which is why we charge a premium for it. It's aimed at delivering on our mission to bring joy and impact back into meetings. In addition to setting up all your meetings, Supercal will help you evaluate them by rating the people in your meetings, by enabling you to stay in touch with key people to get more time with them, and to spend less time with people who don't perform well in meetings or drive it down the path of a bad meeting.

The real magic happens once you connect your calendar and empower Supercal to start analyzing your meetings through research about the people you're meeting as well as optionally studying the transcripts of your meetings, should you enable that feature. We look at the metadata such as the who, what, where, when, and why of the meeting, plus your overall rating of a great meeting versus a bad meeting.

When you call up Supercal, you'll see a list of all your meetings and next to each person you've met with, you can optionally rate them, too. If it was a terrible one-on-one meeting, for instance, you are reminded later not to meet with them again. When you get an email from someone asking for a meeting, we can show you an AI-generated prediction as to whether you would want to meet with this person or not.

Supercal has strong privacy protections, so you can specify who if anyone outside of the attendees can get access to the meeting transcript. Yet for most people, it's not a problem. Millions of people already use AI to transcribe their meetings. While this is comfortable for many people today, some people see this as an invasion of privacy, which is why we built in controls at the individual level.

Yet automatic meeting transcription is already becoming the norm, as most people are already okay with most Zoom calls being recorded. In the future, as soon as people see the benefits of having perfect memory across every meeting they've ever attended, they're going to want their meetings to be recorded.

The benefits of harnessing AI to analyze the meetings are numerous. Supercal can tell you the five action items discussed in a meeting as well as the three decisions made in that meeting. It can also coach you on how to run better meetings and up your ratings by others who've met with you. Supercal does this give you specific feedback: you talk too fast or too slow, you talk too loudly or too softly, you use filler words (*uhm, like, actually*) too often, or you curse too often.

On an organizational level, companies can see which meeting topics are exciting and which are boring their people. What parts of the meeting was everyone paying attention? And what parts of the meeting were people drifting?

We don't want top corporate executives to police the meetings of individual employees. But given that these meeting transcripts could be one the company's largest and most valuable data sets, we want to be able to extract general insights across hundreds or thousands of meetings. You can see if people are aligned with the company's priorities. You can see if people feel aligned with the culture or where they might be struggling. Currently, companies spend a lot of time and money on annual "pulse surveys" to get feedback such as this. Supercal can deliver these kinds of insights on a continual and more granular basis.

All of this brings us back the main thesis of this book: that a strong meeting culture translates into market success and can even lead to market dominance, as achieved by companies such as Intuit, Amazon, Airbnb, Constant Contact, Kayak, LinkedIn, OpenTable, and other top firms discussed as cases in this book.

In the end, better meetings can result in having happier people. As I was completing this book, one of the hottest topics in the workplace being debating online is something called 996, the idea that a company is most successful when its employees are working from 9 a.m. to 9 p.m. for 6 days per week, as this kind of brutal schedule shows true commitment. I think 996 is dangerously foolish.

If you know how to run good meetings and you're making the right strategic decisions, people don't have to work crazy hours. In general, I believe in working no more than 45–50 hours a week for most weeks. At Kayak, even during the heat of launching the website and scaling the service, the number of times I spoke to my cofounder or colleagues on nights or weekends was almost zero. It was probably twice a year. We scaled to 100 million users, billions of searches, and $2 billion dollar sale price—all while working 40 hours or at most 50 per week. For us, working smart was driven by smart meetings.

So far, those individuals adopting Supercal are finding it easy to join this movement of better meetings. But I recognize that there could be challenges or concerns at an enterprise level, which is why I've been speaking at events at companies, everything from lunchtime Zoom meetings to off-site annual conferences. I recently did a fireside chat for Baxter International, which has a mission of "uniting to save and sustain lives." There were 4,000 people on the live Zoom, and then the CEO sent the recording to all 38,000 employees and told them all to watch it. He said I was the highest-rated guest speaker they've ever had. My talk was about more than meetings and focused on where creativity comes from and how to energize teams.

I love doing these sessions, which can incorporate a Q&A discussion on how to best improve the company's meeting culture, and I'm available for more of these kinds of events. And so, perhaps, I may be coming soon to a meeting near you.

Source Notes

The Meeting Book draws its information from original interviews conducted with business leaders, as well as from these prior books, periodicals, and online sources.

Introduction

1. Berenika Teter, Work Meetings in Numbers: Latest Meeting Statistics, Aug. 11, 2025, accessed at: https://archieapp.co/blog/meeting-statistics/.
2. Peter High, Half of All Meetings Are a Waste of Time, Forbes.com, Nov. 25, 2019, accessed at: https://www.forbes.com/sites/peterhigh/2019/11/25/half-of-all-meetings-are-a-waste-of-timeheres-how-to-improve-them/.
3. The Professional and Technical Workforce: By the Numbers, Dept. for Professional Employees, 2024 Fact Sheet, accessed at: https://www.dpeaflcio.org/factsheets/.the-professional-and-technical-workforce-by-the-numbers.
4. What Is the Average Hourly Wage in the U.S.?, Indeed.com, Mar. 3, 2025, accessed at: https://www.indeed.com/career-advice/pay-salary/average-hourly-wage-in-us.
5. World Bank, United States GDP, accessed at: https://data.worldbank.org/indicator/NY.GDP.MKTP.CD.

Chapter 1: How Intuit Became a Master of Meetings

1. Scott Cook interview with the author, April 2025.
2. Hugh Molotsi interview with the author, May 2025.

3. Suzanne Taylor and Kathy Schroeder, *Inside Intuit: How the Makers of Quicken Beat Microsoft and Revolutionized an Entire Industry,* Harvard Business Review Press, 2003.

4. Michael Roberto, Intuit Founder Scott Cook on Experimentation vs. Powerpoint, Nov. 2013, accessed at: https://michael-roberto.blogspot.com/2013/11/intuit-founder-scott-cook.html.

5. Paul English, Ten Things I Learned from Scott Cook, accessed at: https://pme.org/scott.html.

6. Intuit Announces CEO Succession, Aug. 22, 2007, accessed at: https://investors.intuit.com/news-events/press-releases/detail/1145/intuit-announces-ceo-succession.

7. Thích Nhất Hạnh, "Listening Is a Very Deep Practice . . .", accessed at: https://www.azquotes.com/quote/692901.

Chapter 2: How Amazon Revolutionized Presentations

1. Colin Bryar and Bill Carr, *Working Backwards: Insights, Stories, and Secrets from Inside Amazon,* St. Martin's Press, 2021.

2. Texas A&M Stories, How Jeff Bezos and Amazon Changed the World, Feb. 2, 2021, accessed at: https://stories.tamu.edu/news/2021/02/03/how-jeff-bezos-and-amazon-changed-the-world/.

3. CNBC, Jeff Bezos Makes Amazon Execs Read 6-page Memos in Meetings, Apr. 23, 2018, accessed at: https://www.cnbc.com/2018/04/23/what-jeff-bezos-learned-from-requiring-6-page-memos-at-amazon.html.

4. CNBC, Jeff Bezos: This Is the 'Smartest Thing We Ever Did' at Amazon, accessed at: https://www.cnbc.com/2019/10/14/jeff-bezos-this-is-the-smartest-thing-we-ever-did-at-amazon.html.

5. Neal Karlinsky, The Inside Story of How the Kindle Was Born, AboutAmazon.com, Nov. 15, 2017, accessed at: https://www.aboutamazon.com/news/devices/the-inside-story-of-how-the-kindle-was-born.

6. Bloomberg News, Amazon Top Executive Steve Kessel, the Man Behind Kindle to Step Down, Nov. 8, 2009, accessed at: https://www.livemint.com/companies/people/amazon-top-executive-steve-kessel-the-man-behind-kindle-to-step-down-11573263545429.html.

7. Be Bold Digital, Amazon S-Team: The Senior Execs Leading Amazon 2024 & Beyond, accessed at: https://www.bebolddigital.com/blog/amazon-s-team.

8. Marketplace Pulse, Amazon Net Income 2004–2024, accessed at: https://www.marketplacepulse.com/stats/amazon-net-income.

9. Daze Info, Amazon Net Income by Year: 1996 to 2020, accessed at: https://dazeinfo.com/2019/11/06/amazon-net-income-by-year-graphfarm/.

Chapter 3: How Constant Contact and OpenTable Confronted Gender Bias

1. Gail Goodman interview with the author, May 2025.

2. Debby Soo interview with the author, May 2025.

3. Profile of Chef Angie Mar of The Beatrice Inn, Eyeswoon, n.d., accessed at: https://eye-swoon.com/blogs/living/chef-angie-mar-the-beatrice-inn.

4. Get to Know OpenTable's New CEO Debby Soo, OpenTable Blog, Aug. 12, 2020, accessed at: https://www.opentable.com/blog/opentable-ceo-debby-soo/.

5. About Us—OpenTable, accessed at: https://www.opentable.com/about/.

6. What Is the DACI Decision-Making Framework? Definition and Overview, accessed at: https://www.productplan.com/glossary/daci/.

Chapter 4: How Kayak Became Maniacal About Meetings

1. Tracy Kidder, *A Truck Full of Money: Coding, Mania, Love, Genius—The Life of an American Entrepreneur,* Random House, 2016.
2. Paul Schwenk interview with the author, July 2025.
3. Guy Raz et al., How I Built This, National Public Radio, interview with Paul English, Sept. 27, 2021, accessed at: https://www.npr.org/2021/09/24/1040555343/kayak-paul-english.
4. Paul English, Kayak Founding Story, accessed at: https://pme.org/kayak/.
5. Frederic Lardinois, Priceline Acquires Kayak for $1.8 Billion, Nov. 8, 2012, accessed at: https://techcrunch.com/2012/11/08/priceline-com-acquires-kayak-for-1-8-billion/.
6. Mike Damiano, Paul English, the Billion-Dollar Travel Agent, *Boston Magazine*, Jan. 9, 2018, accessed at: https://www.bostonmagazine.com/news/2018/01/09/paul-english/.
7. Web MD, Bipolar II Disorder: Symptoms, Treatments, Causes, and More, accessed at: https://www.webmd.com/bipolar-disorder/bipolar-2-disorder.
8. Paul English, Biopolar Illness and Biopolar Social Club, accessed at: https://paulenglish.com/bipolar.html and https://www.bipolarsocialclub.org/.

9. Charissa Cheong, on Paul English and Bipolar Illness, *Business Insider*, Mar. 20, 2025, accessed at: https://www.businessinsider.com/kayak-founder-paul-english-bipolar-illness-leadership-2025-3.

Chapter 5: How Airbnb Created a New Kind of Company

1. Nathan Blecharczyk interview with the author, June 2025.
2. Belinda Luscombe, Airbnb's Brian Chesky: "The Office As We Know It Is Over," *TIME*, May 8, 2022, accessed at: https://time.com/6174653/airbnb-ceo-brian-chesky-interview.
3. Product releases, Airbnb Newsroom, accessed at: https://news.airbnb.com/product-releases/.
4. Airbnb CEO Brian Chesky Has Banned Emails and Early Morning Meetings, *Times of India*, May 16, 2025, accessed at: https://timesofindia.indiatimes.com/technology/tech-news/airbnb-ceo-brian-chesky-has-banned-emails-and-early-morning-meetings-says-ceos-dont-have-to-be/articleshow/121214215.cms.
5. Steven Levy, Airbnb Is in Midlife Crisis Mode, WIRED, May 13, 2025, accessed at: https://www.wired.com/story/airbnb-is-in-midlife-crisis-mode-reinvention-app-services/.

Chapter 6: How LinkedIn Was Built on Better Meetings

1. Reid Hoffman interview with the author, July 2025.
2. Reid Hoffman et al., *Masters of Scale: Surprising Truths from the World's Most Successful Entrepreneurs*, Crown Currency, 2021.

3. The LinkedIn Story: Origins and Growth Strategy, Startup Savant, Feb. 26, 2025, accessed at: https://startupsavant .com/startup-center/linkedin-strategy-story.

Chapter 7: Transform Scheduling

1. Atlassian Work Life Study, Meet the #1 Barrier to Productivity: Meetings, accessed at: https://www.atlassian .com/blog/workplace-woes-meetings.
2. Lisa Conn, Why Do So Many Teams Still Struggle with Bad Meetings? *Forbes*, Mar. 29, 2024, accessed at: https://www .forbes.com/sites/lisaconn/2024/03/28/why-do-so-many-teams-still-struggle-with-bad-meetings/.
3. Yajush Gupta, Shopify's No-Meeting Approach: Is It Worth Considering for Your Business? Dynamic Business.com, Jan 9, 2023, accessed at: https://dynamicbusiness.com/ topics/workplace/to-meet-or-not-to-meet-the-case-for-and-against-business-meetings.html.
4. Lenny Rachitsky, Shopify CEO on Meetings, LinkedIn Post, Dec. 2024, accessed at: https://www.linkedin.com/posts/ lennyrachitsky_once-a-year-at-a-random-time-shopify-deletes-activity-7275903718523318273-s2Ff/.

Chapter 8: Energize Your Teams

1. Trevor Lasn, The Real Cost of Meetings: What FAANG Companies Do Differently, Sep. 17, 2024, accessed at: https://www.trevorlasn.com/blog/the-real-cost-of-meetings.
2. Dennis Medel and Alex Sherm, Navigating Corporate Etiquette for Global Employee Satisfaction and Retention at Google LLC, ResearchGate, Apr. 17, 2024, accessed at: https://www.researchgate.net/publication/380401959_ Navigating_Corporate_Etiquette_for_Global_Employee_ Satisfaction_and_Retention_at_Google_LLC.

Chapter 9: Meeting Across Cultures

1. Charis Eisen and Keiko Ishii: Cultural Variation in Reactions to a Group Member's Vicarious Choice and the Role of Rejection Avoidance, *Frontiers in Psychology*, June 7, 2019, accessed at: https://www.frontiersin.org/journals/psychology/articles/10.3389/fpsyg.2019.01311.

2. Overcoming Language and Cultural Barriers in Global Teams, Enterprise Workforce Solutions, accessed at: https://www.ews-limited.com/overcoming-language-and-cultural-challenges-remote-teams/.

3. Nathan Blecharczyk interview with the author, June 2025.

4. Stephanie Lynch, 360 Learning, The Power of Shared Experience: How Airbnb Celebrates Diversity Through Multicultural Training, accessed at: https://360learning.com/blog/airbnb-multicultural-training/.

5. Airbnb & Spotify: Case Studies in the Art of Effective Localization, March 28, 2025, accessed at: https://www.gleef.eu/blog/airbnb-spotify-case-studies-in-the-art-of-effective-localization.

Chapter 10: Analyzing Meetings to Make Them Better

1. Ray Dalio, *Principles: Life & Work*, Avid/Simon & Shuster, 2017.

2. Ray Dalio, Principles Online Resource, accessed at: https://www.principles.com/principles.

Chapter 11: Decision Points and Action Steps

1. Scott Cook interview with the author, April 2025.

2. Scott Cook, Culture Change That Sticks, Innosight CEO Summit 2018, accessed at: https://www.innosight.com/insight/scott-cook-ceo-summit-2018/.

Chapter 12: Scaling Meeting Culture

1. Wayne Duso interview with the author, August 2025.
2. Catherine Carlock, Take a Tour Inside Amazon's Newest Boston Office, *Boston Business Journal*, May 15, 2018, accessed at: bizjournals.com/boston/news/2018/05/15/take-a-tour-inside-amazon-s-newest-boston-office.html.
3. *The Washington Post*, 19 minutes with Microsoft's Satya Nadella, Sept. 25, 2017, accessed at: https://www.washingtonpost.com/news/on-leadership/wp/2017/09/25/19-minutes-with-microsofts-satya-nadella-a-new-book-a-new-culture-and-a-complete-nonsense-answer/.
4. Historic Dell and EMC Merger Complete, Forms World's Largest Privately Controlled Tech Company, Dell.com press release, Sept. 16, 2016, accessed at: https://www.dell.com/en-us/dt/corporate/newsroom/announcements/2016/09/20160907-01.htm.
5. Exploding Topics, Number of Amazon Employees, June 23, 2025, accessed at: https://explodingtopics.com/blog/amazon-employees.

Conclusion: Takeaways That Inspired Supercal

1. Paul English, tips on email handling, accessed at: https://pme.org/inbox.html.
2. John Chesto, Paul English's Latest App: A Better Group Calendar, *The Boston Globe*, Sept. 17, 2025, accessed at: https://www.bostonglobe.com/2025/09/17/business/paul-english-supercal-group-calendar.
3. Aisha Malik, Kayak Co-Founder Takes on Calendly with New Supercal Scheduling Platform, TechCrunch, Sept. 16, 2025, accessed at: https://techcrunch.com/2025/09/16/kayak-co-founder-takes-on-calendly-with-new-supercal-scheduling-platform/.

Acknowledgments

I'm deeply grateful to Evan I. Schwartz, my cowriter, whom I spent the last year with, together interviewing about a dozen of the most impressive business leaders I've met during my career. Who would have thought that doing a book about meetings would be such a fun process!

I'm thankful to my team at Supercal, who have taken some of the key concepts of this book and turned it into a product to improve meetings!

I'm indebted to many mentors along the way, including Bill Aulet, Bill O'Donnell, Bill Warner, Brian Kalma, Carol Costello, David Dodson, Deogratias Niyizonkiza, Dharmesh Shah, Eliza Bladon, Fabiola Lopez, Gail Goodman, Giorgos Zacharia, Harry Nelis, Hugh Molotsi, Imari Paris Jeffries, Jack Green, Reverend Jeff Brown, Jeff Rago, Jim Giza, Joe Mahoney, Joel Cutler, Kate Morgan, Kel Kelly, Kimbo Mundy, Krista Pappas, Larry Bohn, Leila Janah, Lincoln Jackson, Reverend Liz Walker, Maurizio Fava, Melissa Fredette, Mike Volpe, Morpheus, Nicholas Lambrou, Ophelia Dahl, Paul Schwenk, Paulina Kusiak Daigle, Peter Kruskall, Petr Kaplunovich, Polina Raygorodskaya, Rachel Neasham, Ralf Boeck, Raman Tenneti, Randal Levenson, Robert Birge, Scott Cook, Stacey Scott, Steve Hafner, Steve Pelletier, Tracy Kidder, Vinayak Ranade, Yasser Bashir, and Youngme Moon.

I could list many things that each person on this list have taught me about business and teams, and about living an inspired life. For those who have since passed away, you remain in my life and in my heart.

About the Author

Paul English is best known as the cofounder of Kayak, the travel search app that was acquired in 2012 by Priceline/Booking.com. The founder of Boston Venture Studio, Paul has launched and successfully sold five other software startups—Lola Travel, Moonbeam, GetHuman, Boston Light, and Intermute.

Paul is also the founder of five nonprofit organizations: Embrace Boston, Summits Education in Haiti, The Winter Walk for Homelessness, the Bipolar Social Club, and the Institute for Applied AI.

While *The Meeting Book* is his first book, Paul is the subject of Pulitzer Prize–winning author Tracy Kidder's 2016 bestseller, *A Truck Full of Money: The Life of an American Entrepreneur.*

Paul grew up in Boston, as did his parents, and his first job was delivering *The Boston Globe.* He is a graduate of Boston public schools and received his BS and MS degrees in computer science from the University of Massachusetts, Boston. Paul is a past winner of the Chief Technology Officer of the Year Award by the Mass Technology Leadership Council.

Index